WILD CHILD – GRO\

Ian Mathie was born in post-war Scotland and spent his childhood and early school years in Africa. After a short service commission in the RAF, he returned to Africa in the 1970s as a rural development officer working with the British government and a number of other agencies. His work in water resources and related projects brought him into close contact with the African people, their cultures and varied tribal customs, many of which are now all but lost. These experiences, recorded in his notebooks, were the inspiration for a series of African memoirs. Ian continued to visit Africa until health considerations curtailed his travelling. He 'joined the ancestors' in May 2017.

By the same author

The African Memoir Series:
Bride Price
Man in a Mud Hut
Supper with the President
Dust of the Danakil
Sorcerers and Orange Peel

The Man of Passage

Keep Taking the Pills

Chinese Take-out

Cover photos

Front cover: *the author, aged two, in Scotland.*
Back cover: *(top left) the author had some of his happiest*
moments flying; (top right) the author entertains his dog
with poems from his collection Keep Taking the Pills;
(bottom) the author at the launch of one of his books with
Andrew Maiden, former chair of Warwick Words literary festival.

WILD CHILD

GROWING UP A NOMAD

Ian Mathie

MOSAÏQUEPRESS

First published in the UK in 2019 by
MOSAÏQUE PRESS
Registered office:
70 Priory Road
Kenilworth, Warwickshire CV8 1LQ
www.mosaïquepress.co.uk

ISBN 978-1-906852-47-4

For Gilbert, McDuff and Harry,
friends who endure for a lifetime

Contents

Foreword: How this book came about

IAN WAS AN ENTERTAINING raconteur and writer who told his true life stories with great vigour and enthusiasm. He had an amazing memory and was able to recall the smallest details of his life even from his early childhood. His life, packed with unusual experiences and adventures in faraway places, strange people, wild animals, danger and fun, was a source of endless fascination for us all – his readers, fans, friends and family.

He had an extraordinary start in life by today's standards. Eventually, he was persuaded to write this book about his early life to answer the many questions about his childhood and growing up in different parts of the world in the final days of the British Empire. He thoroughly enjoyed the process of gathering the material – reading old notebooks, researching dates, unearthing old black-and-white photographs, and recalling his most exciting and dramatic experiences.

Sadly, Ian did not live to see this book in print. He had not quite finished working on it when he was felled by a cerebral haemorrhage, slipping into a coma from which he never recovered. He died on 30th May 2017. Ian's passing was a great shock to everyone who knew him because he had always bounced back before. He was optimistic, determined and fearless, a larger-than-life character who fought cheerfully and won countless seemingly impossible battles with ill health over many years.

A perfectionist, Ian set high standards, insisting that everything was absolutely right when it was really important but tolerant and understanding if things went unavoidably wrong. It is possible he might have made changes to the manuscript if he had lived. But he's not here now to ask so I do hope he would approve of this effort and be pleased with the result.

Pragmatic and realistic, he often used to say: "Don't worry about it. Can't change it now, it's in the past. It's history." How true.

GAY MATHIE
Fenny Compton,
March 2019

A NOTE ON THE PHOTOGRAPHS

Many of the photographs in this book are snapshots from a time before cameras and film were as advanced and affordable as they became. They made their way into the Mathie family albums as a record of times and places and, though technically imperfect, are included here for their relevance to Ian's story.

I developed a mop of carroty curls and a crick in my neck from looking up at people.

1 ~ In the beginning

I SUPPOSE EDINBURGH was as good a place as any for making one's entry into this world, but not in the back of a taxi, as I tried hard to do. In the event, my mother managed to keep her knees clamped firmly together until the taxi delivered her safely to the nursing home in the early hours of a cold, wet April morning. Then everything stopped until after breakfast.

But I'm getting ahead of myself. Let me explain how all this came about.

My father was a soldier and had spent years in India, first with his own regiment, and then on secondment to the Indian Army. He had joined the Highland Light Infantry in Scotland at the end of 1930; early the following year, his battalion was posted to India where he served on the North West Frontier. In 1939, he was sent to Palestine and later to the North African desert, where he was commissioned in the field while commanding a troop of Bren Gun carriers. These were light armoured vehicles – like mechanised wheelbarrows on tracks – carrying a four-man crew and a couple of light machine guns. They moved at up to forty-five miles an hour and proved versatile in the desert.

Dad's left hand was blown apart by a piece of shrapnel in late 1940 and he was sent back to Palestine to have it repaired. Recovering after a spell in hospital, he was loaned to an Indian regiment to command a company guarding a beer stockpile outside Alexandria. He had been chosen for this because he spoke Urdu fluently and got on well with the Indian soldiers. The Indians needed him because they had run out of officers, their own having been killed in battles with Rommel's newly arrived troops. To add interest to the task, he had Australian troops camped on one side of the depot and Canadians on the other, all with a raging thirst for beer. The Indian troops were a Muslim company from the 4/7th Rajput Regiment. They didn't drink alcohol and weren't going to let anyone else near it. In the month Dad was there, they never lost as much as a bottle.

At the end of the month, the Indians asked for Dad to be fully seconded and he was posted to India, to Fattigerh, where he became Brigade Major, despite only being a temporary captain. In this post, he was charged with preparing the regiment to go to Burma, to fight the Japanese.

Dad seized the opportunity to marry the young lady he had been courting since 1932. Molly Wisden was the daughter of a sergeant in his own regiment and had stayed in India when the regiment deployed to North Africa. They married in Rawalpindi on 11 December 1941, going to the high mountains of Kashmir for a brief honeymoon. Soon afterwards they took up residence at No1 Bungalow in the Fattigerh cantonment.

In due course, the Rajput Regiment went to Burma as part of the 5th Indian Division. They played leapfrog with the British 14th Army all the way down through the jungles of Burma, fighting a particularly vicious series of battles against the Japanese between Kohima and Imphal in the spring of 1944. One of these engagements was to raise its head with an interesting surprise at a regimental reunion, many years later in London's Army & Navy Club.

When hostilities ended, the regiment returned to India where he met his firstborn, my brother, Alistair, who had been born during his absence.

Independence was in the air, India was rife with internal rivalry and partition looked like the only way forward. Dad opted to return to his own regiment, which by then was serving with the occupation forces in Germany. En route, he stopped briefly in Scotland to find accommodation for his family.

With my mother and brother settled into a flat in North Berwick, he shipped over to Germany. On arrival, his promotion to Major was confirmed, and he found himself serving as de facto governor of almost a quarter of Germany – quite a position for a man who had joined the Army fifteen years earlier as a band boy with a rifle in one hand and a saxophone in the other. He wasn't even listed as a Private when he was awarded his first medal on the North West Frontier, during the Mohmand campaign. Now he was leading many of the same men with whom he had originally joined up and travelled to India.

His part in the occupation lasted only six months before the regiment returned home. Dad was posted to Edinburgh, with a headquarters office job in the castle. He found the daily commute into Edinburgh impractical and time-consuming, so they moved west of the city to Corstorphine and a third-floor flat in St John's Road. From there, my Mum could waddle to the shops in a few minutes, with my four-year-old brother trotting along beside her. I say waddle because, at the time, she was pregnant – with me.

Few people had a family car in those days, but the Edinburgh trams were efficient and economical. Unfortunately they didn't run in the wee small hours when Mum's labour pains went critical. She'd had a few twinges during the evening, wasn't unduly concerned and felt they'd have plenty of time to get to the maternity unit before anything happened. At about 1.30am, all that changed, and before the hour was out, she was having strong contractions every five minutes. Dad went to the phone box on the corner and called a taxi.

The National Health Service, on which we are so dependant today, didn't exist at the time, so they'd booked Mum into a small city nursing home which specialised in maternity care. It was in Randolph Crescent, close to the centre and within easy reach of Dad's office in the castle.

At 2.30 that wet April morning, as the taxi rattled over the cobbles, Mum's waters broke and the back of the taxi received an unintended drenching. The driver, a big, rough man, was unperturbed. Mum was in good hands, he said – he had delivered his own *bairn* in the back of this very taxi only two weeks before, because his wife couldn't wait. Mum gritted her teeth, clamped her knees together and told him to drive on. However, she did notice from the licence mounted inside the taxi that her driver's name was Iain MacIntyre, and on the dashboard was a familiar insignia, a regimental cap badge for Dad's regiment. That Dad had entrusted her to one of his own men was reassuring.

As the rain pelted down and the taxi skidded around cobbled corners under the sparse streetlights, Mum hung on until they slid to a stop outside a brightly lit doorway. There awaiting her was a nurse, alerted by a telephone call from Dad. He hadn't come in the taxi: fathers didn't routinely attend births in those days, and someone had to stay home to look after my brother. I was clearly destined to be an awkward sod, for as Mum entered the nursing home, her contractions stopped. Nothing more happened until breakfast time had come and gone. When the activity resumed, it came with a rush, and it was all over in a quarter of an hour, five minutes before Dad arrived.

Of course, I don't remember any of this, but Mum made sure I knew all about it as she delighted in recounting the story many times over the years. I do, however, remember some things from my earliest years and our life in the Corstorphine flat.

When I was almost two, just after Christmas, the doorbell rang and Alistair, who must have been nearly six, answered it. He came into the kitchen yelling, "There's a black Santa at the door demanding money."

Mum went to investigate and found a nun from the local convent making her rounds with a begging box. She was raising funds for an orphanage that her order ran in India. In small Scottish communities, everyone knows everyone else's business, so it was public knowledge that Mum and Dad had spent many years in India. The sister obviously hoped this would make them sympathetic supporters, even though we were not a Catholic family. I suspect she was right.

It was cold in Scotland and we saw plenty of snow in my first two winters. I remember Dad and Alistair building a huge snowman in the front garden of our block. It was so well-made it lasted several weeks after the snow on the ground around it had melted, and was a topic of conversation among the *biddies*, who paused to admire it as they passed on the way to do their *messages*.

Once I could walk, we made regular visits to the zoo and to the Edinburgh Botanic Gardens. Each time we went into the greenhouse at the botanic gardens, I would sneak off the path when no one was looking and hide among the plants, pretending I was a jungle explorer. The first time, it sent Mum into a spin when she couldn't find me, but she soon guessed my game and, much to the consternation of the garden staff, we regularly played hide and seek – carefully –among the exotic foliage.

My mop of unruly carrot-coloured curls earned me a lot of attention from the matrons of Corstorphine, and I developed a permanent crick in my neck from looking up at all my admirers.

It wasn't long before the colour faded to blond and my curls straightened out. Then I began to look like a haystack, which was what my brother called me for years. Dressed in my kilt, I still looked a pretty and endearing child (or so I'm told), but whenever anyone told my mother this, she replied, "He might look sweet on the outside, but you don't know the naughty little monster that lives within." Sometimes I think she was only half-joking.

I may have looked sweet on the outside, but inside was something else!

OUR TIME IN SCOTLAND came to an end when Dad was posted to Lusaka as second-in-command of the Northern Rhodesia Regiment. Before taking up his post, he had to do a course at the Royal Military Staff College in Camberley, so we moved south for six months.

Housing around Camberley was impossible to find at short notice and prohibitively expensive, so we rented a semi-detached house in Shiplake, on the Thames, and Dad commuted weekly.

Our next door neighbour in Shiplake was a woman called Edna Harrison. She was unfortunate in having a scrunched-up face with a prominent hooked nose and a large wart on one cheek. She was also the nosiest *biddy* you could imagine. She wanted to know everybody's business and Mum said what she didn't know she'd make up. Her windows were permanently flung wide. If Alistair and I were in our garden, she'd be hanging out looking at us. If anyone came to our door, she'd be leaning out of a front window straining to see who it was and to hear what was being said.

For the very first time, we had a telephone in the house, but it was a shared line. Unfortunately, the person sharing it was Mrs Harrison and naturally she tried to listen in to our calls. Apparently it upset her when Mum's Indian friends called and they'd jabber away in Urdu, with a lot of laughter thrown in.

The village shop was a bit of a communal meeting place for the local wives. One day when Mum and I were in, Mrs Harrison arrived. All conversation died and she stared round scrutinising everyone who was in there. Picking up a tin of sardines, she demanded the price. Mr Williams, the shopkeeper, told her.

"But that's a penny ha'penny more than they are in Caversham. That's profiteering, that is!" She was indignant and spoiling for a fight.

Mr Williams was from the Rhymney valley and had a beautifully lyrical voice. He was unflappable.

"Well, if you want to spend one and tuppence on the bus and go to Caversham, and then one and tuppence to come back, just to buy your sardines for a penny ha'penny less, don't let me stop you. If you go now, you'll just have time to catch this morning's bus at the top of the road."

Mrs Harrison glared at him, slammed her pennies on the counter, snatched up the tin of sardines and stormed for the door.

Outside the entrance to his shop, Mr Williams had some goods on display. There were items like mops, buckets and clothes pegs and, on this occasion, a selection a besom garden brooms. Mrs Harrison turned back from the doorway with one of these brooms in her hand, and demanded to know the price.

"Oh, those are much cheaper here than in Caversham, missus," said Mr Williams. "They're only one and four pence. So shall I wrap it for you, or will you ride it home?"

The whole shop held its breath, waiting for the explosion.

Seconds passed while the village witch digested what our jovial shopkeeper had said, then she wailed, flung the broom down, knocking over a stack of tins, and fled.

When we got home, the house next door was shut up tight. The curtains were drawn and we saw and heard nothing of our bothersome neighbour for nine days. It took the arrival of one of Mum's Indian friends and her husband to break the thrall. Her curtains twitched and were then flung back so she could glare at our visitors.

WHILE WE WERE in Shiplake, Mum's mother died. I had never met my grandmother, nor most of my uncles and aunts, of whom there were about five on Mum's side. There had been a family rift many years before, and they didn't speak to us. At least her parents didn't. Her elder brother had been to visit us briefly in Scotland, but I was too young to remember him clearly. Years later her younger brother, Freddie, who was a dancer with the Royal Ballet, came and stayed with us for a week before he went off on tour to Stockholm. But I'm getting ahead of myself again; more of him later.

Mum went off to Shropshire for her mother's funeral and we boys stayed in Shiplake, where Dad managed to keep us fed with lumpy porridge and burned scrambled egg. There were no freezers or ready meals in those days, so we had to take our chances over food while she was away. An excellent cook herself, Mum always maintained that Dad was the only person she knew who could burn a boiled egg or a kettle of water. So we all had reason to welcome her return.

As summer faded into autumn, Dad's course ended, our trunks were packed, and we made ready to go to Africa. I remember it as an exciting time tinged with sadness: Alistair wasn't coming with us. Since the Army was paying the fees, he was going to a boarding school in Scotland. Dad and Alistair took the train north and my brother was delivered to a dismal school in a small, drab castle at Dalhousie, in Fife. The day after Dad came home, we caught the boat train to Southampton.

2 ~ Outward bound

ON A BLUSTERY LATE September day in 1951, we boarded a ship in Southampton and set sail for Africa. The ship was the RMS *Arundel Castle*, a passenger-carrying mail boat of the Union Castle line, which plied the route to Cape Town and back via Madeira on a six-week round trip, alternating with another ship coming the other way. It was a curious sight: the superstructure was painted brilliant white, while the ship's hull and funnels were pale lilac.

We had a second-class family cabin several decks down from the staterooms. It consisted of a ten-foot-square box with two portholes ten feet above the water. Later, when we were out in a big swell, waves washed up to cover the portholes intermittently with green water, but for now everything was still and calm.

Our cabin was fitted with a double bed for my parents, a wall-mounted bunk for me above the dressing table, and a wash basin on the aft bulkhead. A small wardrobe hung in the corner, by the foot of my bunk; a table and four chairs filled the floor space.

We went aboard just after mid-day, deposited our trunks and baggage wherever we could find space in the cabin and followed

Loading in Southampton: RMS Arundel Castle, *the ship which took us to Cape Town.*

Dad up to an open upper deck. Leaning over the railings, we watched the bustle on the quayside as the ship was prepared for departure. Porters scurried about on the dock, pushing trolleys loaded with luggage and boxes and filling the bulging net of a derrick crane which swung its load up and over the side of the ship and down through a gaping hatch into its bowels.

Amid a chorus of hoots, whistles and shouts, the quay was suddenly no longer beside the boat. It was twenty feet away, and the gap was widening. I remember scampering across to the other rail and watching two tugboats, linked to the ship by straining hawsers, water frothing beneath their sterns, smoke belching from their funnels. They looked small from my vantage point but they were dragging our ship away from the wharf and out into open water. After a few minutes, the hawsers slackened and dropped from the ship into the water. The tugs reeled them in and then chugged off, emitting hoots and puffs of steam from shiny whistles mounted on their smoking funnels.

As the hawsers fell away, the deck beneath our feet, which had so far felt firm and solid, shuddered like a dog shaking itself from nose to tail. The ship began to move slowly forward and we watched the dockside buildings slide past. Before long, we were clear of the docks and out in the main channel. Buildings along the shore looked like toy houses, getting smaller by the minute. As the ship ploughed its way down the Solent, the land slipped away on either side until it eventually disappeared behind us.

I woke up in the early hours wondering why I was being tipped on my head. It felt as if the bottom of my bed was being lifted and lowered, and I had slid down to the head end of my bunk to lie in a crumpled heap. There was a dim light in the cabin, giving just enough illumination to let me see that my parents were asleep in their bed a few feet away, so I was reassured by their presence. Whether things were normal or not, I wasn't quite sure, but I tried to go back to sleep. Even so, the motion kept me awake; from the ship came faint creaks and groans accompanied by a regular swishing sound that was unfamiliar and made no sense to me.

Curtains covered the portholes, so I wasn't able to see outside. Only when morning came and my mother drew back the curtains did I understand what the swishing sound was. Staring out at the heaving grey sea, I watched successive waves roll along the ship, submerging our portholes in a ghostly green for a few seconds as they passed. Added to this excitement, the ship was rolling quite heavily as well, which made it difficult to stand without holding on to something solid.

For the first few hours that morning, Mum looked slightly green herself. She didn't come up to the dining room for breakfast. I didn't understand about being seasick, but Dad said it was something that always afflicted her for the first few hours of any sea voyage. To me, it was all just an adventure, and to have Dad's exclusive company was a treat to be savoured as we explored the ship together. The weather outside was blustery, with flying spray that caught us full in the face when we came round a corner on the open deck. It was exciting, and I wanted to see everything.

Four days later, when the weather settled down and the sea was calmer, it became more exciting still as the crew held a lifeboat drill. We had to put on lifejackets and line up beside our designated lifeboats. The crew threw off the covers and we scrambled in before the davits swung the boats out to hang precariously over the water. They didn't actually lower any of the boats and, to some people's disappointment, they swung inboard again a few minutes later and everyone disembarked. The covers went back on the lifeboats, our lifejackets were stowed, and passengers and crew returned to whatever they had been doing before the drill. In our case, that meant playing deck quoits on the upper deck.

The following day we arrived at Madeira. The port was a smelly place, backed by steep green hills with little white buildings climbing the lower slopes. The quay was too small to accommodate our ship, so we anchored a few hundred yards off and a fleet of little boats shuttled between the ship and the shore, ferrying disembarking passengers and baggage. We weren't allowed off the ship, but I had a wonderful time watching the comings and goings of other vessels, and seeing a giant Empire flying boat arrive and depart. It made a huge and lasting impression on me.

With growling engines it appeared, flying low out of the blue sky directly over us before heading out to sea, where it turned in a wide circle. Coming back towards us, it dropped lower and lower, until barely above the waves. Just as it passed the end of the mole by the outer harbour, it touched the sea, kicking up a huge rooster tail of spray as its hull caressed the water. This lasted only a few moments before the plane settled and growled its way slowly toward a mooring buoy a hundred yards from where we were anchored.

Like ducks coming for bread on a village pond, a fleet of little boats surrounded the great white bird within minutes. I could see passengers clambering out of the plane's hatch and into them for the short trip to shore. Soon a bigger boat approached and attached fuel hoses to the plane. The little boats returned, bringing more passengers.

In less than an hour, the great flying boat sat alone at its mooring buoy. With little delay, the engines coughed, spitting bright flames from their exhausts and belching great clouds of oily smoke before settling to a steady rumble. The engines roared and the seaplane moved off, turning toward the entrance and the outer harbour. Moments later the engine noise increased, spray flew behind the plane and it accelerated toward the horizon. Streaking across the harbour, the great bird lifted out of the water until it was barely skimming the surface, the diminishing tail of spray settling behind it. At last it broke free, rising magnificently into the late afternoon sky, the last of its spray tail dripping from its hull like falling jewels glinting in the sunlight as it climbed. Soon it was a mere speck above the horizon, and then it was gone, heading south to Cape Town, where we too would arrive, ten days later.

OUR SHIP LEFT Madeira some time during the night and we awoke to a long, calm swell under bright blue skies. Somebody reported seeing a whale blowing off, but although we rushed to the rail with everyone else, all I could see was empty sea.

That afternoon I began to feel feverish. By tea time, my skin was blotchy and I was clearly unwell. Mum sent for the ship's doctor who took my temperature, looked at my tongue and prodded my neck. His verdict: German measles. He slapped a large yellow quarantine notice on our cabin door and said I must stay in bed for at least a week, no wandering around the ship.

This was devastating news. The ship was an adventure playground beyond compare. I had made friends with some other children. Together we had taken to clambering over pieces of equipment, climbing ladders on the ship's superstructure, hiding under lifeboats, and generally having a good time.

Now I was trapped in this metal box, with the temperature going up as we headed into the tropics, and all the fun that came with 'crossing the line' no longer in prospect. As if feeling unwell wasn't bad enough, this made me thoroughly miserable.

My parents were attentive and tried not to leave me to suffer too much on my own. They took turns, one going up top while the other staying to read to me, play board games, or try and find other ways of amusing me. But it didn't help much.

After a day of this, they decided they could both go to the dining room at meal times, leaving me alone for half an hour. They promised to bring me back carefully selected food. My suggestion that this should always include ice cream, which I had tasted for the first time in the ship's restaurant, fell on deaf ears.

So at meal times I had the cabin to myself. The first day this wasn't too bad, and I had the promised food to look forward to. On the second day, just after Mum and Dad had gone up to lunch, there was a knock at the door and I saw the handle slowly turning.

The door opened a little and something grey, pink and furry appeared. Whatever it was had my full attention. I sat in bed staring at the strange apparition. Slowly a bit more of whatever it was revealed itself, until suddenly a head came round the door and two huge eyes stared at me. It was an enormous rabbit!

"Hello," said the rabbit in a silly voice. "What's your name?"

I couldn't help giggling, but managed to croak a reply.

For the next fifteen minutes, this wonderful rabbit kept me amused, sometimes talking to me and sometimes talking to someone I couldn't see, who must have been outside in the corridor. Then suddenly it paused, said "Sorry, got to go. See you soon. Bye-bye," and was gone. The cabin door closed and I was left wondering if it had all been a dream.

When Mum came back with my lunch, I told her about the rabbit. She immediately tucked the thermometer under my tongue, opening the portholes to increase the ventilation and turning on the electric fan to make sure I wasn't overheated. She didn't believe a word I said about the rabbit.

During lunchtime the next day, the rabbit came again, opening the door quietly and suddenly popping its head round. This time I saw a bit more of it, and realised it was bigger than me. It was also very funny and told me marvellous stories, interrupted like the first time by asides to someone in the corridor. That someone appeared to be keeping watch.

This time I clearly heard the other voice give a warning that someone was coming. The rabbit said an abrupt farewell and vanished, closing the door quietly behind it.

Once again Mum didn't believe me, however much I insisted I'd had a strange, funny visitor. "So what's its name then, this giant rabbit?" she asked, sounding slightly exasperated.

"I don't know, it didn't tell me," I had to admit.

"It can't have been a real rabbit," she said. "Real rabbits *always* tell you their names."

3 ~ Crossing the line

I WAS AWARE that preparations for some great event were afoot one evening when Dad told me we would be crossing the line the next day.

"What does that mean?" I asked.

He explained that the earth was like a huge ball and the equator was like a line right round the middle of the earth. When a ship crossed the equator, there was a ceremony. Neptune, the god of the sea, would come and smother everyone on the ship in foam, shave all the men, and dunk all the ladies in sea water to make sure everyone was clean enough to go into the southern hemisphere. That was how he kept the world clean, so everyone was getting the ship ready for him to clean it as we crossed the equator the next afternoon.

"Will I get sploshed with foam and shaved?"

"I don't know," said Dad. "It normally all happens on the top deck, but you never know, Neptune likes to make sure every corner of the ship, and everyone on board, is properly clean." I think I caught a twinkle in his eye.

Lunch was early the next day, but a few minutes after Mum

and Dad had gone off to the dining room the door opened as it had the previous two days, and the rabbit appeared, protesting that he was all flustered. This time I remembered what Mum had said and asked him his name.

"Why, I'm Wiggle Nose!" he said. "I thought you knew that. Everyone else does! What kind of a little boy doesn't know I'm Wiggle Nose?" And he had me laughing again in seconds.

I asked if he knew about Neptune and crossing the line.

"Oh yes, that's old hat. Done it dozens of times," Wiggle Nose said. "Mind you, I don't much like all the froth and foam he plasters over you. It makes a mess of my whiskers." Wiggle Nose had particularly fine whiskers. Then suddenly it was "Oops, someone's coming. Bye-bye," and he was gone.

The door had hardly closed when it burst open again. I expected Mum with my lunch; instead it was a huge man. He had a crown of curly red hair and a big bushy beard, all tangled with seaweed. A tattoo of a mermaid with a green tail covered his chest. His trousers appeared to be made of scaly green fish skin and he had paddles for feet. In one hand, he carried a bucket filled with white foam, and in the other he held an enormous paintbrush.

"Ho-oh, it's time for a good scrub, my boy," his voice boomed as he approached the bed dipping the brush in his bucket of foam. Before I could protest, he had slathered foam all over me and was roaring with laughter. I didn't know whether to laugh or to cry, whether to be afraid or think it was a huge joke. Before I could decide, he produced a big soggy sponge and wiped the foam off my face, leaving streams of salty water to dribble onto my bunk. It was soon awash.

"There you are," the big voice said. "You'll do to cross the line today. Get better soon; I want to see you on deck before this ship reaches port." With that he picked up his bucket and left, leaving me sitting in a soggy pool of foam and seawater. I didn't know what Mum was going to say when she came back with my lunch.

But it was Dad who arrived. He looked at the chaos in the cabin and guessed immediately what had happened. The foam wasn't just on my bunk, I now realised; the man had splashed it all over the place – great dollops on the floor, the small table under the porthole and even around the porthole. A strand of seaweed dangled from the open lip.

Dad laughed. "So, you've been sploshed and scrubbed, have you?" I told him what had happened. "Yes, that was Neptune all right," said Dad. "It's a pity he makes such a mess, but then I suppose living at the bottom of the sea he doesn't mind having water and seaweed all over the place."

He bundled up the soggy bedding, used our towels to dry the plastic-covered mattress and anything else that needed it, and dumped everything outside the door. "We'll get more sheets later, when things quieten down," he told me.

Dad explained that he and Mum had to go up to the top deck for half an hour, but they'd be back soon with some special cake. I noticed him collect both their swimming costumes before he left, but thought nothing of it.

Ten minutes later, the door opened again. It was Wiggle Nose and he was covered in white foam.

"My goodness that was a narrow escape; that Neptune's a wild one," he panted "I thought he was going to shave all my whiskers off with that great big razor he's got! He's never been like that before. I see you got done. First time was it?" And for ten minutes we giggled together until the voice in the corridor warned him someone was coming. He vanished in the usual manner.

Mum and Dad came back together, both looking like they too had been thoroughly foamed and scrubbed or dunked. The cake was every bit as good as I'd hoped. It even made up for my having missed the ceremony. After all, I'd had a private visit from the sea god and I'd seen Wiggle Nose twice – and Mum and Dad still thought I was making him up.

They didn't believe me until the sixth day.

That day Mum had been flustered by something before going up to lunch and must have chosen to come back in the middle of the meal. Anyway, Wiggle Nose was in full flow when I heard the voice in the corridor saying "Ssshhh! There's a sick boy in there, and we're trying to cheer him up. After all, he's missed all the fun up top."

"I know, he's my son," I heard Mum's voice say.

"Cor, lumme," the other voice said. "Well, don't tell anyone. We're just trying to help."

There was more chat, but it was too muffled for me to hear, and Wiggle Nose was doing a great job keeping me laughing. He stayed a bit longer that day, but eventually the door closed behind him. About half an hour later, Dad arrived with my food. The doctor was with him and insisted on examining me before I ate. When he was finished, he expressed himself satisfied and said that after one more day of confinement, I could rejoin the rest of the passengers. By that time we would be nearly at Cape Town.

4 ~ Cape Town and a train ride

IT WAS LATE MORNING when the ship docked in Cape Town. As we were military passengers, we disembarked last. So we stood by the rail on the top deck, watching as two smoky, hooting tugboats pushed the ship the last few yards to the quay.

The dockside was bustling with people. Between the gangway and the doorway into a huge shed that all passengers had to pass through to enter South Africa, hawkers had set up a line of market stalls. Most were selling wooden carvings, leatherwork, beaded bags and other unidentifiable handicrafts. A few stalls were stacked with fresh fruit, flowers and vegetables, looking colourful and exotic in the sunshine.

As we watched, a man in a white suit and a straw hat bustled down the gangway against the flow of porters coming aboard to help disembarking passengers with their baggage. He went over to one of the stalls and began what looked like a furious argument with the trader. After a few minutes of arm-waving, he gave the trader some money and the trader passed something to him. The man in the white suit headed back to the gangway. Now passengers were disembarking, so again he had to push and barge his way against the flow, finally disappearing through the large opening in the side of the ship. A few minutes later the man in the white suit appeared at the top of the companionway to the upper deck. He looked around and strode purposefully in our direction. When he reached us, he bent down to my level and held out the object in his hand.

"Hello Ian." It was the voice I had heard in the corridor. "My friend Wiggle Nose tells me you've been sick and confined to your cabin for most of the trip. He asked me to give you this to remember him. It was supposed to be a rabbit, but they don't seem to have any rabbits here, so he hopes a tortoise will do instead." He pushed a small black tortoise into my hands.

"Thank you very much," I said politely, then asked: "What's your name?"

"I'm Terry Thomas," he said with a cheeky grin. "I'm glad to see you're better, but I must dash. I've got to get my crowd to the theatre." With that he was gone.

"See, I told you there was a rabbit," I said to Mum. I didn't mention that I'd heard her talking to Terry Thomas outside the cabin door until many years later. By then I realised he was a famous English comedian and character actor. I named the tortoise after him, and that's how he has been known ever since.

My ebony tortoise has been known as Terry Thomas ever since.

EVENTUALLY IT WAS our turn to get off the ship. With a trail of porters bringing our luggage, we made our way across the dock to the immigration desk just inside the large shed. The formalities were brief and a few minutes later, we emerged from the other side of the building to where a train stood waiting. The carriages were brown and cream, with Rhodesian Railways emblazoned along their tops.

We couldn't see the engine from where we boarded, and it was only later when the train reached some long sweeping curves that we could see the great puffing monster that was pulling us, smoke billowing from its funnel.

Our carriage had a corridor along one side and was divided into twin berth sleeping compartments. Each one had a hanging wardrobe and a small wash basin in the rear corner, with transverse bunks set above one another on the forward wall. Most of the fourth wall opposite the compartment door was a big window. You could lower it completely to pass in luggage so you didn't have to struggle along the narrow corridor with it. Since the compartments were meant for two people, and there were three of us and lots of baggage, we had two adjacent compartments allocated to us. Mum and I were to sleep in one, and Dad occupied the next one. He had to share with the luggage, which took up a whole bunk and half of the floor, but during the day he sat with us.

After all the bustle and efficiency on the dockside, it seemed to take ages before the train was loaded and finally started moving. Eventually there was a series of jolts and we crawled out of the docks and through the edge of the city.

On the corridor side, the land rose towards a huge flat-topped mountain, the fabled Table Mountain. Out of the compartment window, we could look out over the sea. I soon lost interest in the

Mum and I on the train at Cape Town, waiting to depart.

passing scenery, explored the compartment and made myself at home. We were going to spend the next three days in this train, so it paid to know where everything was and how it worked.

Little boys love exploring and fiddling, and I was no exception. I soon figured out how the fold-up bunks worked. Then I managed to spill water all over the floor by turning on the taps in the wash basin. It turned out that the drain wasn't connected to any pipework so it needed a bucket underneath to collect waste water. I also discovered I wasn't strong enough to raise or lower the large window on its heavy leather strap.

In a compartment at the other end of our carriage was a family with a little boy whom I had got to know on the ship. After frequent trips along the corridor, from one compartment to the other, we began to explore further afield and discovered the restaurant car.

It was late afternoon when the train left the docks, and it seemed like we had hardly left the city behind before it started getting dark. Before long the world was completely black outside. All we could see was a scatter of twinkling lights where there were houses, and pale grey streamers of smoke from the engine, illuminated by light from the carriage windows.

We must have gone along to the restaurant car for supper, but I have no recollection of it. Before long it was time to lower the bunks and install myself in the top one. I slept soundly. The next thing I remember is Mum waking me for breakfast. She had raised the dark blind which covered the window the night before and flooded the compartment with golden sunlight. It was warm too.

Breakfast was a delight, with piles of fresh fruit and big bowls of cereal. Most of the fruit was new to me, and I wanted to try everything. Mum knew better, and let me try only one new thing at each meal. It was a clever way of making sure I was keen to get to the table, but also saved me from a case of the trots. After our somewhat restricted diet in post-war Britain, where some rationing was still in force, my stomach wasn't yet accustomed to the rich varieties on offer.

In the Britain we left behind, fruits such as pineapples, mangoes and *naartjies* weren't commonly available. In fact, for me pineapple had only ever come in small chunks, sealed in tins of sickly sweet juice. I liked *naartjies* which were exotic citrus fruits, similar to oranges but not quite as sweet, with less pith under the skin. They were also easier to peel. Their novelty and pretty name added to the attraction they held for me.

At lunch and in the evenings there was meat, more meat, and even more meat – more than we were used to. Yet it seemed to be the bulk of what people ate here. It was only after we arrived in Lusaka and were settled into our house that I discovered this was not the case; most local people lived on *sadza*, made from ground corn cobs, or *posho*, a kind of millet porridge. Meat was a luxury.

The countryside that first morning was wide and open, broad

rolling sweeps of grassland, dotted here and there with small clusters of huts and occasional clumps of trees, or small rock outcrops. As the day wore on, the rock outcrops got bigger until we passed some spectacularly large craggy edifices. There were small fields with crops growing in neat rows, interspersed with broad areas of grassland. Spindly flat-topped trees dotted the countryside. Long-horned cows grazed in closely grouped herds, watched over by little naked boys waving long sticks.

The train maintained a steady pace but it wasn't travelling very fast and it tended to go slower when we came to any sort of a gradient. Just before dark on that first full day, we came to a sprawling town of dusty streets and shiny tin roofs. Some buildings stood alone; others had gardens with spreading trees bearing scarlet flowers and pendulous black seedpods.

Occasionally we passed a tree that looked dull and almost dead, standing eerily skeletal and alone, bearing tufts of leaves at the tips of its grey branches. Clusters of white or pink flowers adorned some branches and long pendulous pods hung from others. These were trees I would come to know well and discover all sorts of good uses for, encountering them all over the continent during the years ahead. They were baobabs, called by the Africans the tree that God turned upside down, because their grey leathery trunk and branches, devoid of foliage for most of the year, looked more like roots than branches.

Our carriage was near the back of the train, and as we went around a long curve, I was excited to see its length stretched out before us. There were now two locomotives pulling us. Each had a tender, laden with wood, and we could see men tossing logs forward to fuel the engines. A slight breeze carried great billows of white smoke from the engines' funnels off to one side.

That afternoon Michael, the boy I had met on the boat, told me we would reach our destination the following day. He suggested we ought to make marks in our compartments, to claim them as our own. Even at that age, I had a little pocket knife so, while sitting on the floor supposedly playing with a Dinky Toy, I used it to scratch my mark on the underside of the metal washbasin in our compartment.

Almost fifty years later, I was to discover that same carriage in David Shepherd's railway museum at East Stoke, in Somerset. When I bent down to check the washbasin, I was delighted to find my mark still there.

Soon after breakfast on the third morning, the train slowed and came to a stop in a cloud. Looking out the window, we realised we were on a bridge and the cloud was in fact spray. It was accompanied by a deep rumbling sound. Dad opened the window to lean out and see where we were, but soon closed it again to prevent everything in the compartment from getting wet. A few moments later, we saw a man outside with a brush, attacking the train. Dad risked lowering the window again for a moment to ask what was going on.

"The crew are scrubbing the train," he announced as he hauled the window shut by its leather strap. He was bedraggled and soggy from where he had been hanging out to get a good view. "This is Victoria Falls. We've stopped on the bridge, and the crew are using the spray to wash off all the dust we collected crossing the veldt."

After about half an hour, the train moved off and we left the spray and the thunderous rumble of the falls behind. Coming out into the bright sunshine, we could see the length of the train on a curve. It looked like new. Later I asked our carriage steward why they had washed the train that way on the bridge. "The water of *Mosi oa tunya* is free," he told me, "and it washes better than hosepipes."

Mosi oa tunya, I learned later, means 'Smoke that thunders'. It seemed a particularly apt description and was my first introduction to the lyrical names Africans give both to natural phenomena and to people who have distinctive qualities.

After the Victoria Falls wash down, we stopped briefly at Livingstone, where a number of passengers disembarked, my new friend Michael included. The train rolled on, passing through increasingly frequent patches of verdant cultivated land. As the sun descended towards the western horizon, we pulled into Lusaka station. In the excitement of reaching our destination, I soon forgot Michael as many new encounters and experiences filled the days and weeks that followed.

Mosi oa tunya *as we could see it from our carriage window just before the bridge.*

5 ~ A new start in Lusaka

AN ARMY LAND ROVER and a 15cwt truck were waiting to meet us at Lusaka station, together with a young British officer and several *askaris*. The *askaris* piled our baggage into the truck, which immediately drove off in a cloud of dust. We climbed into the Land Rover and the officer drove us to the military cantonment, pointing out and identifying buildings and other places in the town as we passed them. He finally pulled up in front of a white building with a thatched roof. This was to be our new home.

The house was set well back from the road and appeared to have a few bushes and trees around it. In the gathering darkness we could see little of the garden. There would be plenty of time to explore tomorrow, I was told, as we were ushered into the house.

Outside the front door waited three men who looked like soldiers. They stood to attention in a line, all dressed in smart khaki uniforms with black fez hats, puttees round their legs, and bare feet. The officer who had collected us introduced them. Corporal Gideon Chilomo was to be our cook. He was a round smiling man of about forty, built like an ox and quietly spoken. Lance Corporal Samson Mulaya was Dad's batman, looking after his uniforms and running any military errands he might require. Samson had a slight limp, but was smart and efficient and, as I was to discover later, a man who had distinguished himself as a soldier.

The third man was simply named as Nkoti. Although he wore the same uniform as the others, he was given neither rank nor family name, and I was never entirely clear about his status. He turned out to be a jack of all trades; part house steward, part gardener, part general handyman. Nkoti was also the guardian of the regimental mascots: four crested cranes, which lived in a pen at the bottom of our garden. He had a lugubrious face which made him look as if he was carrying the cares of the world on his shoulders but, as I learned over subsequent weeks and months, he was a gentle soul with a wealth of knowledge and skills which he was always willing to share.

I was up early in the morning, eager to explore our new home. The house itself was a mud-walled bungalow, white painted with a thatched roof, deeply overhanging eaves, and cement floors painted red. There were no ceilings in the rooms; we looked straight up into the thatch. It was cool and airy, with one electric light dangling from the rafters in each room. A wide drive with rocks scattered along its margins swept up to the front of the house from one pillared gateway and curved back to the road through another. Like all the roads here it was just graded earth, showing ruts where wheels had carved its surface during recent rain.

The large front garden had once been carefully laid out with shrubs and flowerbeds, but now looked neglected because the house had been unoccupied for three months. Mum had been telling us on the train how much she looked forward to having a proper garden. She'd always managed to grow things wherever we lived, and often talked about the lovely plants she'd enjoyed so

The house was standard colonial design – a mud-walled bungalow with thatched roof and large windows that made it cool and airy inside.

much in India, long before I was born. So although the garden was still quite green, I knew it would soon look very different.

The kitchen was at the back, in a separate building, joined to the house by a short covered walkway. Beyond that was a small vegetable plot, carefully cultivated and growing things I didn't recognise. To one side, behind the kitchen, stood four round huts with conical roofs, partly screened from view by large leafy bushes. Although all were neatly whitewashed, three of the huts looked slightly scruffy and untidy. They were the staff quarters, where Gideon and his family lived. The fourth, used as a washhouse and batman's pantry, was where Samson washed and ironed Dad's kit and polished his boots. It was as smart as the man himself.

The ground sloped away from the house at the back and, about fifty yards further on, I discovered an area surrounded by a tall mesh fence. This immediately intrigued me and I wanted to know what it contained. Walking round outside the fence, I could see bushes and clumps of tall grass, but no obvious reason for the enclosure until I reached the furthest corner. There I found a small open shelter. Standing in front of this, pecking at a dish of food, stood four majestic birds. Their backs were a dark grey, with white and rust-coloured wings folded low over a rusty rump and short dark tail. Their long necks were covered with streaky silver-grey plumage, topped by a scarlet bib. Black and white heads carried short beaks like daggers and each wore a spectacular golden crest. Standing taller than me, the cranes had slender grey legs with wide splayed toes, which folded together as they lifted them delicately to stalk about their enclosure. All four heads turned in my direction as they became aware of my presence, but soon dropped to their food when it was clear I presented no threat.

These were the regimental mascots, and over the next three years I would spent many happy hours standing outside their enclosure observing them, drawing them, and learning that they weren't nearly as delicate as they appeared. These birds were tough customers, not afraid of taking on snakes, scorpions, rats, or any other birds that tried to steal their food. Even Nkoti, who had looked after them for years and knew their ways, was wary of their sharp beaks and slashing claws.

We spent the first few days unpacking our trunks and trying to make the house feel like home. Although furnished with a standard military issue of beds, chairs, dining table and so on, it was still a bit empty until our main baggage arrived at the end of the second week. An army three-ton lorry drove up to the front door, carrying nine huge crates and six grinning *askaris*. With a lot of laughter and chatter, they soon had the boxes unloaded and deposited in the house. The boxes were all numbered and Mum knew precisely where she wanted each one put. One of the *askaris* produced clippers and a screwdriver with which he cut the steel banding that secured each lid and removed the retaining screws. As soon as this was done, the lorry and its merry crew departed, leaving us to unpack.

Unpacking was a task my mother liked to do herself, without help, so I was sent out to amuse myself in the garden. I wandered down to look at the cranes again and after a few moments was joined by a small boy about my own age.

"Hello," I said.

"*Bwanji*," he replied.

"My name's Ian."

He looked confused.

"What's you name?"

He looked more confused, his big eyes staring at me as if I were something strange – which, to him, I probably was.

"Ian," I said again, pointing at my chest. Then I pointed at him and raised my eyebrows, holding out my hand.

"*Dzina langa ndi Robat*," he said, finally getting the idea and holding out his own hand.

"*Dzina langa ndi Ian?*"

"*Inde!*"

I shook his hand and said, "Nice to meet you."

He pointed to the birds in the pen and said, "*Zingaru.*"

I repeated the word.

"*Awdgalu*," he said, holding up one finger. "*Nayi zingaru*," he held up four fingers.

"*Zingaru?*" I enquired, holding up two fingers.

He grinned. "*Eye, viri zingaru.*"

My first lesson in a new language.

Robert turned out to be Gideon's third son, and we soon became firm friends. Whatever we lacked in a shared language soon ceased to matter as we learned new words from each other while we explored the bush behind the compound. Within a few months we would be going to school together, along with his big sister, Sunday, and more of Dad's soldiers' children.

After the great unpacking, there was a lot of social coming and going, meeting the other expatriate officers' families, and getting to know our way around. At first we were confined to places within walking distance in the military cantonment, unless one of the other wives invited us to accompany her to town, as we didn't have a car. Then Dad arrived home one day in a black Ford he had bought from an old wartime friend, Charles du Vivier, a Belgian tobacco farmer who was going home to Ghent on leave and intended to bring a new car back with him.

Our horizons extended.

Coming to Northern Rhodesia meant we adopted English instead of Gaelic as the family language at home, as that was what everyone else spoke and we needed to fit in. It was easy enough for Mum and Dad, but meeting all these new people was a bit of a strain for me because my English was minimal. It hadn't often been spoken at home, so I hadn't learned much more than Robert had. Most of the other expatriate children were a few years older than me. The language barrier made making friends a clumsy process and the older European children soon got fed up with trying, but one girl, Vanessa Bunn, who was my age, was very friendly and faithful. Her father was one of the company commanders who had served with Dad before, just after the war. She was one of the few white children I had any time for.

Most of the other families with young children employed a local woman to act as *ayah* and mind their children. Mum didn't see the need for this as Nkoti and I had made friends from the first day. He was a calm, unflappable man, and Mum decided he could keep an eye on me for such extra attention as I needed. Her decision shocked some of the other mothers, but it suited us.

TIME FLIES WHEN you are young and before long preparations for Christmas began. Whenever we appeared to have nothing to do, Mum organised Robert and me to glue strips of coloured paper together to make colourful chains. We festooned the house with these and the passageway out to the kitchen. This caused Ruth, Robert's mother, to hoot with glee. She soon had us making paper chains to decorate her *rondavel* as well. Paper lanterns appeared as if by magic from Mum's secret store, and over a couple of weeks the house gradually took on a festive air. We couldn't find any holly because it didn't grow here, but substituted other pretty leaves, most of which went limp and shrivelled within a day or so of being picked. Still, the bush behind the back garden was verdant and greenery was soon replaced. The bush was also full of interesting life forms like cicadas, ants, stick insects and praying mantises, with gave me endless interest.

We were not the only ones getting ready for the festive season. We heard there was to be a big celebration among the troops in the barracks, with dancing and music. The excitement mounted daily, and long before Christmas it was at fever pitch.

On the day before Christmas Eve, in the middle of the afternoon, I was standing by the pen looking at the crested cranes when the air started to throb. At first it was no more than a subtle vibration, like the distant rumblings of thunder. Yet the sky was clear and there was no sign of rain. This background rumble grew slowly and developed a rhythmic pulse. A musical quality became apparent as its intensity and volume increased. Robert came rushing down the garden to find me, calling me to come and see. The dancers were coming. He grabbed my hand and pulled me back towards the house, round the end of the building to the front drive.

As we skidded to a stop, I saw a hideous sight approaching from the front gate. Hundreds of strange figures were coming down the drive, bouncing with every step, their bare feet stamping in unison, stirring up the dust, their voices chanting resonant responses to the calls of their leader. They had almost no clothing on; the little they did wear appeared to be made from strips of skin and animal tails. Each man carried a large oval shield and a sharply pointed spear, which he thumped against the shield in time with the steps. As panic rose in me, I barely had time to recognise any of the faces, although one or two appeared to be slightly familiar.

I was terrified. They were devils!

Without thinking, I tore my hand from Robert's grasp and fled in through the front door. Desperate for somewhere to hide and get away from these devils, I rushed into my Dad's dressing room, dived into the big press where his clean uniforms hung and pulled the door tight behind me. Cowering behind the smartly pressed clothing, I slowly slid down to squat in the rear corner, piling his shoes and boots in front of me to make it more comfortable and add to my concealment.

The chanting and stamping outside still reverberated, but it seemed less threatening in here. If I couldn't see the dancing devils, they couldn't see me. I was safe in my hiding place.

I must have fallen asleep for I woke up with my legs cramped and a crick in my neck. Memory of the terror I had come in here to escape flooded back. It made me cautious about movement and making any noise. Everything sounded quiet outside, but I knew I had to be careful. They'd been making a lot of noise before, but devils like that could be sneaky, and I knew they had been after me. They could be out there still, waiting for me to give my position away, ready to pounce the moment I revealed myself. I moved carefully to a more comfortable position, rolling onto my side and resting my head on a pair of soft suede mosquito boots.

Time passed. I must have slept again, for the next thing I was aware of was Dad shaking me, saying it was safe to come out now.

Morning sun streamed in through the window. Everything was quiet. Dad was dressed in a check shirt and tan slacks. He pulled the hanging clothes aside, helped me to my feet, and kept hold of my arm to help as I climbed unsteadily from the press.

"Have those devils gone?" I asked timidly, ready to dive back into the dark recess if his answer was no.

"It's all right," he assured me. "They've gone." He led me to the bathroom and wiped my face with a damp cloth, then ruffled my hair, saying "Come and have some breakfast."

At the mention of food, my stomach rumbled. I hadn't realised how hungry I was. But then I hadn't eaten since lunch the previous day, and normally had a voracious appetite. Mum was putting cereals and fruit on the table as Dad and I took our places. Nothing was said about my vanishing trick as we ate.

Afterwards, laden with swimming gear, towels and sun hats, we set off to the camp swimming pool to join all the other officers' families, before going to an open-air lunch party at the club.

I hadn't learned to swim yet, but enjoyed splashing about in water. Next to the main pool there was a shallow one for the younger children and non-swimmers like me. As I sat dangling my legs over the edge of the pool, I began to understand that I might have made a fool of myself by running off and hiding like that. Despite my limited English, I could understand enough to realise that everyone else had been delighted by the dancers who had scared me so much. People were talking about their performance with enthusiasm, saying they were impressed by the dancing and the soldiers' singing. They were looking forward to the next time.

Not making any sense of this, I resolved to ask Robert as soon as we got home. He had already become my best friend, and my mentor in all things African.

I found Robert down by the cranes' pen later that afternoon. Half expecting him to be cross with me, I apologised for running off and leaving him to face the devils alone.

"Not devils," he replied. "*Askaris*. My father was the *induna*!" he was obviously very proud of his dad.

Remembering that some of the faces had looked familiar, I began to realise why. Not only had Gideon been the leader, dancing in front of the others, but Samson and Nkoti had been in the line-up too. Robert explained to me that this was a traditional greeting. The dancers were soldiers, dressed in their traditional tribal style. For dances like this, their tribal captains led them. They had come to salute my Dad.

Understanding this made me feel really foolish and realise I had so much to learn.

6 ~ New Year, new adventure

THE NEW YEAR BROUGHT another adventure: school. Our Belgian friend Charles du Vivier was well acquainted with the sisters at the mission near his farm, and said they ran a good school. My parents had already looked at the army school and found it wanting, so one morning they left me playing with Robert and went to visit the mission school. Although we were not Catholics, both Mum and Dad were enthusiastic about Sister Bernadette who had shown them around, but sounded a little less keen on the Mother Superior, perhaps because she was German. Having fought them in the North African desert during the war, and had his left hand blown apart by a bit of their shrapnel, Dad didn't like Germans on principle. Thinking about it years later, this – and a similar dislike of Japanese, against whom he had fought in Burma – were the only expressions of prejudice I ever heard my Dad utter. He usually liked and got on well with everyone, even when he had to be the disciplinarian.

Putting his prejudice aside, Dad said the school had been very neat and tidy, the children all seemed happy, and their standards were good. He and Mum had agreed to send me there when term started in two weeks. They never mentioned that I would be the only white child there: all the other white army children either went to the camp school or, if they were older, were sent back to Britain to boarding schools. They did, however, tell me that a lot of the soldiers' children – many of whom, like Robert, were now my friends – would be going to the mission school. An army bus would take us all together each morning, and bring us home in the afternoon. The school day was from eight in the morning until two, with a break for lunch.

Before that, we had to get through New Year and all its attendant festivities. The soldiers came around again to dance in formation, dressed as before in their tribal garb, singing and shaking the ground with their rhythmic stamping. This time I knew what was going on, and looked out for the familiar faces. Sure enough, Gideon was in the lead, with Samson and Nkoti close behind. This time I marvelled at the movement and the resonant voices, my feet subconsciously picking up the rhythm.

Before I realised what was happening, Robert had grabbed my hand and dragged me forward to join the line. I didn't need much encouragement, and I could see by the broad grins of the dancers I knew that I was welcome. When the formation moved on to visit other officers' houses, Robert and I went with them. My parents waved us goodbye.

When we eventually got back, I sat down to eat *sadza* and *msuzi* with Gideon and his family, my parents having gone out to an official party to welcome the new commanding officer, Colonel Goode. Tired and full, I fell asleep in a heap with the other children, which was where Gideon's wife, Ruth, found me in the morning when my parents were awake and asking for me.

That afternoon, the soldiers Beat Retreat on the parade

ground. It was an impressive display, and familiar because I had seen similar parades in Scotland, yet somehow it held less appeal for me than the vibrant tribal dancing of the previous afternoon. That had a fluid motion about it, the voices of the singing warriors were joyful, their energetic rhythm compelling. This was stiff and stylised, the men's voices silent, the regular tramp of their studded boots slightly muffled by the grass and the music from the band, punctuated only by the occasional barked order.

The ranks of soldiers were impressive in their stiffly pressed khaki uniforms, black fez hats, black boots glistening, and the bayonets on their rifles glinting in perfect symmetry as the columns wheeled to march past the saluting dais in long, straight ranks. But in Scotland, the Highlanders had looked far more exciting in their swinging tartan kilts, cockades in their hats, the massed bagpipes skirling and a big bass drum thumping out the pace that echoed back off the surrounding buildings. There just seemed something elemental about their performance which was missing here.

DAYS RUSHED BY. Suddenly the first day of term was upon us. As Mum and I walked down through the barracks, exchanging greetings with other army wives sending their sons and daughters off to school for the first time. Dozens of parents and children gathered around the khaki-painted bus parked outside the main barracks, chattering and excited.

Robert hadn't come with his mother. His big sister, Sunday, had already been attending the mission school for two years, so she was entrusted with his care. Ruth had also told her to look out for me. In the excitement, I didn't even stop to say goodbye to Mum as I climbed into the bus and found a seat among the merry crowd. It was only years later that I thought about what she must have felt that day.

The mission school was some miles from the army camp, which was on the edge of town. Before long, we were heading out into the countryside along one of the few metalled roads. A few signs dotted the roadsides. Signs were beginning to have meanings for me: I had learned my letters from sitting on Dad's knee and following his finger as he read his newspapers. I was beginning to recognise words and copy them with a stick of charcoal. One particular sign became a landmark. About two miles out of town, it was a large red triangle above the words 'Beware of Africans'.

I didn't understand what it meant. Neither did any of my friends sitting near me, but it made us laugh. We wondered if we would see another sign saying 'Beware of British' on the way back.

The mission school was three low white buildings with bright wriggly tin roofs and large windows. They looked out over a courtyard shaded by three huge mango trees, laden with unripe fruit. We stared at them as the bus drew to a stop, dreaming of the day when the mangoes would be ripe, hoping we might be allowed to pick and eat some of them.

Our daydreams were interrupted by the appearance of stiff figures shrouded in long white robes. Five nuns, their heads crowned with stiffly starched wimples, their faces unsmiling, small wooden crucifixes dangling on chains from their necks, approached the bus in a phalanx.

The nuns ushered us off the bus, pushed us into two lines and told us to be silent. They then started calling our names out and we were supposed to respond. The little girl in front of me must have been stung by an insect as she suddenly squealed and began slapping her bare legs. I was so distracted that I didn't hear my name called. Suddenly a hard bony hand gripped my left ear and twisted. I screamed and received a whack round the other ear.

"*Chele salondola*," the nun snarled. I cowered.

The sister taking the roll called my name again.

"*Inde!*" I croaked as my ear received another savage twist between the nun's fingers when my name was repeated.

The nun calling the register glared at me and moved on down her list.

They divided us into three groups and herded us into separate classrooms to sit on hard wooden benches. One of the sisters stood in front of us and explained how school worked. She spoke in Chinyanja and, as I was not yet fluent, I understood less than a third of it. Sitting next to me, Robert gave me a nudge me and whispered, "Just do what I do."

Salvation.

This advice turned out to have a major drawback as a few minutes later Robert did something wrong and received a clip round the ear. Copying him, I received the same punishment. Neither of us had noticed the second nun standing at the back of the class. I never understood what we'd done wrong, but we all soon learned that retribution for any misdemeanours, be they real or imagined, was instant and savage.

By the time we got on the bus to go home, I wasn't sure I liked school. I certainly didn't like the nuns. My protests fell on deaf ears with Mum and Dad, who said I had to give it a chance. It was only because everything was new and unfamiliar. It would all settle down. I wasn't convinced.

Of course it did settle down, or at least I learned to accept the system. But I never learned to like the nuns. They were cold, hard women. Most were Germans and Italians and, although they spoke Chinyanja fluently, they all had funny accents. This caused us lots of amusement, even if it did result in clips round the ear when we sniggered.

Sister Bernadette was the exception. She was the one nun we all liked. She was Irish, quite a bit younger than the others, and she was warm and friendly. She loved children and we all loved her. She also spoke Gaelic, so whenever I couldn't understand the Chinyanja I could turn to her with some hope of comprehension as our two languages were similar.

The Mother Superior was Sister Esmerelda, a stiff, sour woman of about fifty, with a pinched face, a sharp pointed nose and beady little eyes set too close together. With a face like that, she reminded us of a mongoose, and soon became Sister Monguus to us army brats. A rigid disciplinarian, she also had a cruel streak that didn't fit easily with her supposedly Christian calling. Even the other nuns were inclined to be tense and edgy whenever she was around.

Most of our instruction involved chanting in unison, repeating whatever the teacher had just sad. We learned our letters and numbers this way, those of us who hadn't already learned them chanting along with those who had. A routine soon developed that was based on the progress of the slowest and it didn't require much effort to keep up. Provided one was seen to be chanting along with everyone else, there were lots of opportunities for other diversions.

Robert and I soon made friends with another lad, Gilbert Chileshe. His dad was the regimental sergeant armourer. When we got off the bus back at the camp, Gilbert would often come and explore the bush behind the house with us. He soon changed his seat in class so that the three of us could sit together. When the lesson was boring, we amused ourselves by passing things we had found in the bush back and forth, making girls in the row in front squeal by putting grasshoppers on their hair, and other naughty things. The chaos we managed to cause was worth the occasional smacked ear and, amazingly, the nuns never thought to separate us. Perhaps they thought it was easier to keep all the trouble in one spot.

AFTERNOONS WERE adventure time. First the three of us went down to the pen to inspect and admire the crested cranes. While these statuesque birds seldom did anything spectacular, we always wanted to check on their well-being. Besides being the regimental mascots, they had become a talisman to us. By their mere presence they assured us all was normal in the world. Mostly they simply strutted about their enclosure, pecking at insects, seeds and anything that looked edible. Otherwise they just stood and watched us watching them.

Occasionally one of the cranes would spread its wings to perform a brief erotic dance. Contrasting with their stiff golden crests and red bib, the black, white and russet plumage on their wings was dramatic, and the movement was guaranteed to attract attention. Sometimes two birds would dance at the same time, a duet mating performance, accompanied by sharp cries from the birds and squeals of delight from us. On one occasion all four cranes performed together. This was magical.

We didn't spend all our time watching the cranes – there were lots of other things to do, and plenty of bush to explore. Ant heaps provided a lot of entertainment as we watched long lines of tiny insects carrying food back to their nest, and occasionally used

Crested cranes dancing.

a stick to brush some aside, breaking the flow. We also discovered that there were different sorts of ants, all looking quite distinct and ranging from little red fire ants, well named because their sting felt like being burned, to the huge soldier ants, over an inch long and marching in determined ranks.

Ants provided us with endless hours of inventive amusement, and more than a few stinging bites. Trying to pick a single ant out of the column, which was often a dense stream six inches across, became one of our regular games whenever we located soldier ants. We considered catching a single one and confining it to a match box or jam jar an achievement of heroic proportions. Not getting bitten by it was another.

We regularly found things like lizards, snakes and chamæleons in the bush. Neither Robert nor Gilbert were keen on touching any of these, and were more inclined to throw stones at them. Snakes they hated and feared. Both were at first alarmed when I picked one up, screaming at me to drop it as it was poisonous and would kill me if I got bitten. Having caught it, letting go sounded dangerous, so I hung on and carried it homewards to ask Nkoti what I should do.

Nkoti was surprised to see what I was holding and declined to come too close, waving me away as he backed off himself.

"Dis one bery bad snake," he spluttered. "He bite you, you die."

"So what can I do with it?" I asked.

"You muss cut him neck," he drew a knife and made throat cutting gestures."

"But I don't want to kill it."

"Den you muss break him teeth, so he no bite," he said, gestured against his own teeth to show how I should attempt this. He laid the knife on the ground and scuttled out of the way as I bent to pick it up.

While all this was going on the snake had wrapped itself around my arm and was squirming to free itself. Adjusting my grip on its neck, I prised its mouth open and swept the blade across its fangs, feeling a crunch as they snapped. Venom spurted from the snake's mouth and its black forked tongue licked the air.

Nkoti told me to point the snake's head into a dark place under a pile of sticks and release it. With its body still tightly coiled round my arm, this sounded risky, but I had to try and there was no way I could unwind it. I stuffed the hand holding the snake's neck under some sticks, relaxed my grip, and waited for the bite. It never came. Instead, the snake relaxed its grip on my arm and it flowed smoothly away into the undergrowth.

Robert and Gilbert had followed all this from ten feet away, ready to run at any moment if the reptile escaped my grasp and turned in their direction. Now they looked on in amazement as I stood up, safe and unbitten. My stock was high with them at that moment because I had picked up and handled a poisonous snake, and survived. If we were inseparable before, this cemented our relationship.

All the same, I was still the new boy here, and both Robert and Gilbert had a lot to teach me.

The patch of bush behind our house was on the edge of the army camp. It wasn't that wild, but it was full of adventure. It sloped gently downhill almost a mile toward a small river. Beyond the river lay fields of maize, millet and sugar cane, with small clusters of round huts, the homes of farming families. We often went down to the river which, while definitely flowing, was sluggish and muddy. Even so, its water was cool on our feet and it wasn't long before Robert and Gilbert shed their shorts and jumped in. I did likewise, making sure I didn't go in too deep because I couldn't swim. It was as we climbed from the water, naked and dripping, that Gilbert pointed at me and said in an awed tone, "You've been circumcised!"

"So?"

"We don't get that until we're ten. It's part of the initiation ceremony done by the *nganga*," Gilbert said.

I looked at my friends and, sure enough, they both still had foreskins. Although I didn't really understand why, it was clear that my missing foreskin gave me status. My standing with my friends increased a notch.

The following day, a strange man appeared when we went down to look at the cranes. He said nothing to us, but stood some distance off, watching us. Gilbert noticed him first and nudged me.

"What does he want?" I asked.

"To see you. My dad will have told him; he is his brother."

"Told him what?"

"You're already circumcised. Among our people, the only ones who have this early are special."

"So why should it matter to him?"

"Because he is the *nganga*."

I was unsure what this meant, but it made me feel slightly uneasy, so I stopped asking. After about five minutes, the man turned and started walking away, disappearing from view in an open space where there were no bushes to hide behind. It was as if he'd just evaporated. We all saw it, but none of us could explain how he did it.

Beyond our garden there was no village in a formal sense, although a number of villagers lived there. Everyone in the neighbourhood belonged to the same clan of the same tribe and, as time passed, we got to know them. A few worked in the army camp and one or two of the children came to the mission school.

Exploring the bush helped us learn about many sorts of plants. There were those whose bark made good string; grasses with sharp edges that sliced through skin like a sharp knife if you were unwary enough to run a hand over them; leaves which could be rolled into instant cups and containers; and plants with resinous sap which could stick things together. It was a wonderful playground, somewhere with limitless interest, potential and resources.

The bushes were home to a variety of birds, from exotic blue rollers and shrikes, to tall storks and cranes, and tiny jewel-like sunbirds that flitted between the flowers on bushes and trees.

There were mammals as well and these included dik-dik, a diminutive antelope, mongoose, and several varieties of rats, mouse, bushbabies and small carnivores. Their tracks were easy to find, but the animals themselves were shy and often nocturnal.

One of our favourite games was catching *chongololos* – millipedes, big black things, eight or nine inches long and as thick as a man's thumb – and seeing who could roll a coiled one furthest. When you picked one up, they would coil into a tight disc which you could roll along the ground. Normally the moment they came to rest they would uncoil and try to scuttle off, so you had to be quick to pick them up again. The game was not without its hazards: the *chongololo* had a nasty bite that hurt at the time and – swollen and infected – for days after as well. Getting bitten taught us to be more careful. It was a lesson that proved valuable to me throughout many years living in the bush.

7 ~ Tobacco, mambas and mealies

DAD HAD MET UP WITH his old friend Charles du Vivier at an official function soon after we arrived in Lusaka. Charles had returned to Belgium at the end of hostilities, only to discover that the family brewing business was too restrictive an environment for him after all the excitement he'd had overseas. Needing to stretch his wings, he decided on a new adventure, bought a farm a few miles outside Lusaka and planted tobacco and *mealies*. These were good cash crops, and Sheko Farm was doing well, with the tobacco being sold profitably overseas and the *mealie* crop going for local consumption.

We were regular weekend visitors at Sheko Farm, where there were lots of opportunities for adventure for small boys. Apart from farming, Charles was a keen polo player, and kept a stable of ponies. When we visited, the adults would go riding together in the farm's thousand or so acres of fields. I stayed around the farmstead with the du Vivier children, who were slightly younger than me, in the care of one of the farm staff. We were never at a loss for things to do and spent happy hours running up and down the rows of crops in the adjacent fields, the aromatic tobacco plants standing taller than our heads.

The *mealies* too were tall, their big fat cobs waving silky tassels in our faces as we patrolled the rows looking for cane rats. We didn't find many and they were usually too swift for us to catch unless we laid snares. One thing we didn't expect to find, and which gave us a bit of a fright, was one of Africa's more poisonous snakes, the green mamba. They were quite common in the sugar fields, where they climbed the canes to catch finches and other small birds that lived in the tall foliage. Workers cutting sugar cane frequently encountered them at head height, which made work in the cane fields hazardous.

For some reason, a few had migrated into the maize, possibly finding the cobs gave them a better purchase for climbing to the right level to catch the small *quelia* birds, which regularly pillaged the crop. *Quelia* were like little red-beaked sparrows and lived in huge flocks. When the *mealies* were ripening, Charles deployed a full-time gang in the fields to scare them off with bangers, rattles and loud gongs.

When I came in from the *mealie* patch one Saturday morning with a live five-foot green mamba in my grasp, the farm hands wouldn't come near me, insisting I kill it immediately. I didn't want to kill it, so we had a standoff that lasted nearly an hour until the adults returned from their ride. When Charles saw what sort of snake I'd caught, he explained that there was no safe way of releasing it. He told me to hold its head over a large stone, and then he hit it hard, once, with another stone. The mamba's head turned to mush and its long thin body twisted in knots for a few seconds, before it relaxed and lay still.

As we stretched the corpse out to measure it, Charles

explained to me why these snakes were so dangerous. Dealing with things like this every few days, and being responsible for his workers' safety, he had studied them and understood how the snakes lived and hunted. His explanation had my full attention and quickly converted my disappointment at its death into interest about how different types of snakes lived. Seeing that he had fired my curiosity, he promised to teach me more about these slippery reptiles.

A few weekends later, he took me on a snake hunt, showing me the habitats each one preferred and how to recognise the signs of their passage and the presence of concealed snakes. Each time we found a new snake, he showed me how to identify, catch and handle the species safely.

Charles was about to throw the dead mamba into the rubbish pit, but one for the farm hands came and asked if he could have the snake. I asked why he wanted it and Charles said it was probably because the man was a bit of an *nganga*. He would use it to make traditional medicine.

"What does being a bit of an *nganga* mean?" I asked.

"It means he's only a part-time witch doctor," Charles explained. "The rest of the time he's my tractor driver and mechanic."

I looked at the man carefully and realised I'd seen him before. He was Gilbert's uncle, the man who had come to stare at us when Robert, Gilbert and I were down by the crested cranes' pen the day after we'd been skinny-dipping in the river.

THE TOBACCO HARVEST was a busy time. Charles's workers hung the leaves on long racks in huge drying barns. Each barn contained ten double-sided racks about a hundred feet long. They were open at each end so the air could flow through and dry the tobacco evenly. The big leaves were hung individually, upside down by their stalks on nails driven through the wooden rack so that their points protruded as sharp prongs. The sides of the building were boarded with planks and the roof was made of wriggly tin with a layer of thatch on top, to stop it getting too hot inside. The tin was there to stop insects or other wildlife from dropping out of the thatch onto the leaves.

Workers continually walked up and down the rows of drying leaves, checking their condition. As they dried, the tobacco leaves lost their soft green colour, turning a pale brown, shrinking slightly until they reached precisely the right degree of dryness. When the leaves were ready, workers packed them in huge bales which were wrapped in oiled brown paper. Most of the leaves were dried *au naturel*, but a few batches were dunked in a weak solution of water and molasses before they were hung up to dry. If there was any sign of insect infestation, a light dusting with sulphur might be applied; smoke from second-rate leaves smouldering in a canister also got rid of bugs. All these treatments produced different smelling tobaccos by the time the leaves were baled and sent to market.

Another source of great fun was the *mealie* harvest. There were no fancy machines for this in those days. Every cob had to be removed from the stalk and striped of its husk manually. The farm workers were experienced hands, *mealies* having been part of their staple diet for generations. Working their way along the rows, cutting down the stalks, removing and stripping the husks, they left behind small piles of naked cobs. Later, as a tractor towed a trailer slowly down the field, many willing hands collected the *mealies* and tossed them into the trailer. Picking up and tossing the cobs was hard work, usually accompanied by a lot of chatter, singing and laughter. It was easier for children who didn't

On top of the mealie *pile at Sheko Farm.*

have to bend so far, so the farm workers' families came to join in and speed up the work, earning a few extra shillings and a bag of corn for their contribution.

By the time a ten-acre field had been cleared, our arms ached. The full trailer returned to the farm and added its load to the growing mountain of *mealies*. The next step was to pass them through a decorticator machine to strip the grain from the cobs, ready for drying and milling.

The best bit for us was seeing the huge heap of *mealies* our work produced, and climbing on top to play king of the castle.

I noticed that the tractor-driving *nganga* watched me carefully every time I climbed the *mealie* mountain. I was now sure he was the same man who had stared so intently at Robert and me down by the crested cranes' enclosure. Although Alistair too climbed the *mealies*, the man never took the slightest notice of my brother. As before, it was slightly disconcerting to be the centre of unspoken interest, but I didn't feel in any way threatened.

8 ~ Horses

BEFORE WE'D LEFT ENGLAND, we had made a family outing to Battersea Park in London, to visit the Festival of Britain Pleasure Gardens. The highlight of the day for me was a ride on a Shetland pony. At Sheko Farm I got another chance to ride a horse, and soon developed a liking for it. The horses were friendly and calm, and while I wasn't initially allowed to ride free, there was always someone around to hold the bridle or a leading rein. It was hardly surprising, then, that I spent as much time as possible on a horse, with or without a saddle. It didn't take long to gain proficiency. Mum was a good rider, having always had horses in India, and took every opportunity to join me. It wasn't long before we were able to go off for rides together.

During the later holidays, when my brother was with us, he came to Sheko Farm too. He didn't like horses, wasn't keen on riding, and preferred to clamber over the farm machinery and imagine himself driving smelly tractors and mending broken machines. Whenever Mum and I went riding, he disappeared into the farm workshop.

Riding opened new horizons and extended my range to the

*Astride a Shetland pony at
Battersea Park.*

farthest fields on this huge farm. If none of the adults was riding,
Adam, one of Charles's grooms, was generally delegated to
accompany me and took great delight in showing me out-of-the-
way corners and special places where we could gather wild figs,
mangoes or *mupfura* fruits that grew on three huge Marula trees.
Occasionally there were enough ripe fruits on the ground for us to
return to the farm with a basketful.

We occasionally saw wild animals on our rides. These were
mostly small antelope and gazelles or porcupines and the occasional aardvark that had surfaced in daylight. Aardvarks are normally nocturnal, but could sometimes be seen around dusk as they
set out on their nightly foraging expeditions. They also had the
awkward habit of digging huge holes in the farm roads and tracks.

This wasn't a big game area; most of the more recognisable
game animals like zebra, buffalo, wildebeest or other antelopes
and the big cats, giraffe and elephants kept clear of the cultivated

lands. We did, however see lots of birds and a quite a few snakes. Adam was always reluctant to stop and look at snakes, having heard about my habit of picking up venomous reptiles. On one occasion, when I was about to dismount to examine a large puff adder we had discovered, he gave my pony a mighty whack on the rump which made the beast take off at speed with me half out of the saddle and clinging to its mane.

He told me later that the *nganga* had told him that morning not to let me touch a snake. I wasn't sure whether he was more scared of the *nganga* and what might happen if he disobeyed him, or of any serpent I might chance to pick up. He'd already seen me handle several snakes and knew I could do it safely.

Riding one of Charles du Vivier's horses at Sheko Farm.

9 ~ First safari

AS THE END OF the first school term approached, Dad announced we were all going on safari during the holidays. Alistair, who was still at a boarding school in Scotland, was flying out to join us. He would arrive four days before the end of term.

I was excited about his arrival, looking forward to showing him my favourite spots in the bush, and introducing him to my new friends. I was intensely disappointed to have to go to school on the Tuesday morning, while our parents went to Lusaka airport to meet his plane. The word was out among my friends that he was coming, and we all listened carefully for the aircraft's arrival. None of us had a watch, although we all knew how to tell the time by the passage of shadows across the classroom floor. Gilbert suggested we hold a competition to see who could predict exactly when the aircraft would pass overhead. We scratched lines on the polished floor in front of our bench to indicate where the sun coming through the window would have reached when the plane flew over.

Shibolo, who sat next to the window, was appointed as lookout. When he saw the plane overhead, he was to hiss and we would then check our lines to see whose was closest to the shadow cast by the window frame. Robert won – and Shibolo got a slap round the head from the watchdog nun for hissing.

On that day in particular, school seemed to drag on interminably. To relieve the boredom Gilbert handed me a cricket he had caught outside during the mid-morning break and secreted in his shirt pocket. After examining the insect, I put it in the hair of the girl seated immediately in front of me. This caused a few giggles from the boys either side of me and a few moments later, when the girl realised what I'd done, she shrieked and started batting at her hair. Her outburst brought the nun from the back of the room down on us, slapping our ears and shouting at us to behave, then dragging Gilbert and me out to stand facing the corners at the rear of the class. It was our bad luck that it was Sister Ursula: she had the boniest hands and she wielded them with vigour and force. Our ears would sting for days after a whack from her.

When we finally got home, I rushed ahead leaving my friends to follow. My excitement turned to disappointment when I found there was nobody at home. The place was deserted. I went round the back to find Nkoti, who told me my Dad had gone back to work, and Mum and Alistair had gone off somewhere in the car. By this time, Robert and Gilbert had arrived, so we wandered down to stare at the crested cranes in their pen. The birds just stood and looked back at us, not even bothering to peck at anything on the ground. They were boring when they behaved like this, but they looked as if they too were waiting for something exciting to happen.

Eventually the sound of the car returning brought us scurrying back to the house and I was able to introduce my two friends

A coiled up chongololo.

to my big brother. Big was a very suitable description as he had grown at least six inches since we had last seen one another four months earlier. He now stood well over a head taller than me, and I was bigger than either Robert or Gilbert, despite being younger than both of them.

There was so much I wanted to tell and to show him that it was difficult for Alistair to get a word in at first. Eventually, after sitting and drinking large glasses of orange juice, Mum suggested we take Alistair down the garden to see the crested cranes. We all trooped out, but never got to their pen because on the way I saw a *chongololo,* and dived into the grass to catch it. Once it was safely coiled up, I offered it to Alistair, thinking he would like to see it at close quarters and try rolling it along the ground.

With it tightly coiled between his fingers, he stood there uncertain what to do with it. Before he could decide, the *chongololo* began to uncurl itself, twisted into a corkscrew, and fell to the ground. Not wanting my trophy to escape, Alistair made a grab for it, managed to catch hold of the middle of its body, and got his finger bitten as it coiled up again. That put a stop to our expedition as he ran back to the house, yelling that he's been bitten by a black monster. Robert, Gilbert and I looked at one another and shrugged. The *chongololo*, cast aside when it bit his finger, had disappeared into the grass.

Alistair's swollen red finger throbbed for three days before the pain subsided. He declared I was nothing but a hateful little savage, playing with such dangerous toys, and was wary about touching anything I offered him for the rest of the holiday. He was a bit tentative with my friends too, and it took me a few days to realise that this was because, isolated in rural Fife, he had never seen black people before he arrived in Lusaka. What I took for granted, ignoring the minor difference of skin colour, appeared new and more than a little strange to him. It took him a long time to understand that we were all the same inside.

On the last day of term, Alistair came on the school bus with us. Mum and Dad had something they needed to do together and there was nobody to look after him. Ever since his arrival, he had protested loudly about how much he hated his school in Scotland. He asked why he couldn't be here with us, and go to the same school as me. Mum and Dad decided he should come and see my school, and then figure it out for himself. It didn't take long for boredom to set in as he sat on the bench, swinging his legs, unable to understand a word, and wanting to be somewhere else.

After about half an hour, the nun teaching us said we must sit quietly and wait. She had to go and fetch something. As soon as she left the classroom, Alistair walked to the front of the class, picked up the chalk and began drawing on the blackboard. He didn't hear Sister Monica return, but she saw him. She stopped in the doorway and watched as he concentrated on his drawing. His lines soon took shape and the figure of an *askari* emerged. The whole class sat in silence, watching, occasionally glancing at Sister

Monica to gauge her reaction. To our amazement, she actually smiled. When he had finished, she patted him on the shoulder, telling him in broken English that it was a very good drawing. Then she dismissed the class, saying that since it was the last day of term, the bus was taking us home early. There was an instant noisy stampede for the door.

As I passed the blackboard, I took another look at my brother's drawing and noted the *askari* he had drawn bore a remarkable resemblance to Samson. I marvelled momentarily at his ability to capture an image with a few lines before hurtling on to claim my place on the bus.

NEITHER ALISTAIR NOR I clearly understood what going on safari meant, but it was clear we were going somewhere in the bush, and would see lots of big animals like giraffes, antelopes called *kudu*, and buffalo, maybe even lions. Exactly where we were going to stay was never explained, but I noted there was no tent among the kit we had spent a day collecting.

By bedtime, the car was packed with everything except the food we would need for the journey, and our washing kit. My excitement lost out to exhaustion and I soon fell asleep. I woke to find Alistair shaking me, saying if I wanted any breakfast, I'd better be quick as everyone else was ready to go. I was out of bed, into a pair of shorts and stuffing my face with fruit and cereal in less than two minutes.

Dad explained that we were going to a place near the Kafue River. There was a Game Park there and the ranger, a man called Gerry Taylor, was an old friend of his from their time together in Burma during the war. He had invited us to stay in his house, and would show us around the park.

It was a long way west to Kafue, and would take us two days to get there, depending on the state of the roads. We were going first to Mumbwa, where we would stay in the government rest house overnight, carrying on across the Kafue River to the park the next day. This really was going to be an adventure.

It wasn't long before the tarmac surface petered out and the road became a dirt track. At first it seemed smooth enough, but soon we encountered corrugations. Little ridges ran across the road, creating a surface like a wriggly tin roof. These made the ride uncomfortable unless you were going at just the right speed for the car's tyres to skip over the crests. Go too slowly and the car juddered as if about to shake itself to bits; too fast and there was the risk of skidding off the road into the bush. Since there was a storm drain as deep as six feet on either side, going off the road was likely to be calamitous to say the least.

We'd been travelling about three hours when we got our first puncture. Mum decided it would be a good time to have lunch while Dad changed the tyre, and proceeded to produce a picnic like a magician pulling rabbits from a hat. She had a small folding table and groundsheets for us to sit on. Alistair decided he would prefer to sit on a fallen log, a few feet from where we stopped. I warned him to be careful, but he said it was solid and quite safe to sit on. I hadn't quite meant that, but he was still cross with me over the *chongololo* bite and wasn't going to take any notice of anything I said. Two minutes later he was dancing around like a lunatic puppet with ants in his pants. I bit my tongue, trying not to laugh, and had time to notice a brief smile on Mum's face. She understood. She'd spent time in the bush when she lived in India and knew all about ants. She also knew that I understood the hazards. The bush was, after all, my playground.

Back on the road, with Mum driving, we made good progress. We came to a section of the road that had recently been graded and was free of corrugations and potholes, which meant our ride was a little more comfortable. It was not, however, free of hazards. Cows stood on the road and seemed reluctant to move for an oncoming car. We even saw a large bull elephant, which ambled slowly across in front of us. He wasn't getting out of the way for any mere car.

Mum was able to maintain a good speed and the miles rapidly disappeared in the long cloud of yellow dust that followed our progress. After a couple of hours, she stopped to change places with Dad, and to let us all stretch our legs. Mumbwa was only about another half hour's drive.

We had barely got going again before Dad was standing on the brakes and pushing himself back in his seat. A gaping chasm across the full width of the road drew nearer with sickening speed as our locked wheels slid on the dusty road and the rattling old car fishtailed alarmingly, tossing us from side to side on the slippery leather seats. There were no such things as seat belts in those days.

We juddered to a halt skewed across the road, barely five feet short of toppling into the chasm.

The hole stretched from one side of the road to the other, with rough edges and steep sides dropping at least three feet below the road surface. There had been heavy rain a few days before and it appeared this had caused a culvert under the road to collapse. The roadway here was supported by wooden beams which had been eaten by termites. Vibrations from vehicles had weakened the rotten, half-eaten wood; long hours of tropical rain made the soil too heavy, and the culvert gave way.

From the absence of wheel ruts, it looked as if there hadn't been any traffic since it had happened. We would either have to fill in the hole, or bypass it to get any further along the road.

It now became apparent why Alistair and I had been travelling with a shovel and a hoe beneath our feet in the back of the car.

We were about to start digging, intending to build ramps down one side and up the other, when Mum pointed out that the surrounding countryside was rising. A few hundred yards ahead, the storm drain petered out. If we could get the car level in the ditch to our left, with one wheel on each side of the drain, we could drive along until it came level with the road and then carry on. All we needed was a single ramp down. Alistair may have been only nine years old, but he got the idea immediately and soon proved his skill at wielding a shovel.

We took turns at digging to make a diagonal slope into the ditch and in less than an hour, it was done. Dad inched the car down the ramp and turned along the drain. In five minutes he had made it to level ground and our car was back on the road. Smothered in dust but happy, we put the shovel and hoe back on the rear floor and climbed gratefully into our seats.

Darkness was almost upon us by the time we reached Mumbwa and found the rest house, where the steward had a meal waiting. I don't remember what we ate, but it had been a tiring day and my bed called me.

Dad went into the town the next morning to find someone who could repair our tyre. In those days, tyres all had inner tubes which, when punctured, had to be removed and patched. It was quite a performance and often resulted in further punctures if the inner tube got pinched between the wheel rim and a tyre lever while it was being levered back in place.

He came back with a long face. A local garage had repaired

the tube, but warned him that it had already been repaired a number of times, and needed replacing. Unfortunately nowhere in Mumbwa stocked that size of inner tube. The best Dad could do was buy a bicycle tyre repair kit, and hope the repaired tube would last until we got back to Lusaka.

It didn't. Half way between Mumbwa and the Kafue River, where we were due to meet Gerry Taylor, we got another puncture and had to put the repaired wheel back onto the car. It lasted ten miles before this one burst again. Dad managed to get the tube out from the first punctured tyre, in the hope of using the bicycle kit to repair it, but found that none of the patches in the repair kit he had bought was big enough to cover the hole. Propping the car up on the jack and leaving the wheel in situ, he began levering off the rim of the tyre that had just blown. He removed only one side, and then began pulling handfuls of grass from the roadside and stuffing them inside on top of the burst tube. We all joined in collecting grass to keep him supplied until he'd stuffed the whole tyre full.

He levered the tyre back onto the rim, lowered the jack and we drove on for a mile. Then we stopped, jacked up the car again, levered open the tyre, and stuffed in a load more grass on top of the first lot, which after a mile had been well compressed. Dad forced more and more grass inside, using the tyre lever to poke it in until it felt hard. Once again he levered the tyre back behind the rim and lowered the jack. We had to go slowly, but it worked, and we only had to stop once after that to stuff in more grass before we reached the Kafue River.

We arrived later than intended, but Dad's friend and two of his rangers were there waiting for us. Realising we had been delayed, they had been off and shot a young buffalo that now lay on a large trailer hitched to the back of his Land Rover. This carcass was to provide meat for all the staff at the park centre, and we'd have a piece of it for supper tonight.

But what to do about our broken wheels? Dad suggested transferring all our kit into the Land Rover and leaving the car until we could come back with mended tyres. Gerry thought this was a bad idea. If we did that, the car would be turned into metal utensils in no time. By morning, people from nearby villages would have stripped every panel from the car to beat into all sorts of useful containers, plates and household goods, both for their own use and to sell in the market. The seats would disappear to someone's house deep in the bush, to give comfort to a few old men as they sat chattering, and the car would be no more than a skeleton by the time we came back, even if it was only this time tomorrow.

Gerry suggested another solution. He removed the tail board from his trailer and backed it up close to our car. Then, while Dad, Gerry and the two rangers lifted the front of the car, Mum reversed the Land Rover. When the front wheels of our car were firmly onto the trailer, they let the car down and secured it with the blood-soaked ropes Gerry and his men had used to haul the dead buffalo onto the front part of the trailer. They hooked a steel cable from the winch at the front of the trailer to our front suspension and pulled tight so the car couldn't slide off backwards.

Once Gerry was satisfied, we climbed into the Land Rover, the two rangers sat on top of the buffalo carcass, and we headed for the park centre at twenty miles an hour. It sounds simple, but was inevitably a little complicated because first we had to cross the Kafue River. Although not fast-flowing, it was sixty yards wide and too deep to ford. The ferry was a flat-topped barge made of empty oil drums with planks on top. This floated across on a cable and was only just big enough to carry our strange vehicular combination. Not to be deterred, and with his rangers watching the sides, Gerry drove onto the ferry as if he did this with unusual loads every day of the week, stopping with his front wheels inches from dropping off the front of the barge.

The ferry lurched and rocked as the current pushed us sideways, sloshing water over the sides, but we made it safely across.

After crossing the river, we travelled on a well-maintained game park road, and our rate of progress improved. Even so, it had been dark for half an hour by the time we reached the ranger station. A crowd soon gathered and helped lift our car from the trailer. By the light of a Tilley lamp, others took hold of the buffalo, knives flashed and before long the beast had been skinned, cut into pieces and distributed. Gerry's cook took a large lump to prepare for our supper.

When Dad went out to look at our car in the morning, he found it propped up on blocks. The park's mechanics had removed all four wheels and taken them away to do something about our tyres. They didn't have any spare tyres the right size in their store, but said they had a solution. We found out later that they replaced all four wheels, and the spare, with wheels off another old car which had an exploded engine and wouldn't be going anywhere for a long time. Its wheels were a slightly different size from ours, but by drilling new bolt holes in the wheels and with a bit of bashing to expand our mudguards, they were made to fit our car.

African mechanics are infinitely inventive. We left them working on it while Gerry took us out in his Land Rover to see the game park.

10 ~ Animals and strange men

THE KAFUE GAME PARK included vast open spaces of sparsely inhabited countryside. Although it had become a protected area only a few years before, it teemed with animals. Within an hour of leaving the centre, we had seen eight or nine different species of antelopes. The biggest was a huge sable bull, his thick curved horns sweeping back like dark scimitars above a rich dark brown velvet coat. His contrasting pale cheeks and belly lent him an impressive appearance. Although he stood quietly, staring at us as we drove slowly past sixty yards away, his massive shoulders and strong haunches gave the impression of great power. His gaze followed us until we had reached some magical distance where we could no longer be a threat. He wasn't an animal to challenge.

At the other end of the spectrum, and far more plentiful, were little Thomson's gazelles. These dainty creatures wore a broad black waterline stripe along each side of their slim khaki bodies and down each cheek. They were fine-lined and graceful; a group of them in motion appeared to flow like bubbling water over a stony stream bed. Their herds merged with other antelope grazing their way across the open savannah.

When we encountered a group of zebra, I was delighted. They looked so smart in their black and white striped coats, and snickered and squealed when excited or surprised. Jobi, the ranger who sat in the back of the truck with us, said the locals called them 'Donkey wearing football jersey', which seemed a suitable name. I had seen pictures of convicts in striped uniforms, so I told him the zebras looked like horses escaped from jail. He laughed so hard he fell out of the truck and had to run hard to catch up and scramble back on board. From that moment, Jobi became my favourite ranger and my friend.

We stopped in a village where Gerry needed to talk with the headman. It happened to be the village where Jobi's brother lived, and Jobi offered to show Alistair and me around. He took us first to his brother's compound where his relatives made us welcome and gave us fresh bread to eat. It was unleavened, dry and stodgy, but similar to food I had eaten at my friends' houses in Lusaka. Alistair was accustomed only to Scottish baking and didn't like it. He took one bite and passed the rest to me. Alistair also had the disadvantage of not understanding a word that was said, whereas I had by now gained some proficiency in the local language and could at least observe the courtesies and make out the gist of anything we were told.

We went to another compound and sat in the shade watching a strangely dressed man who was talking rapidly in another language. He looked remarkably familiar, but I couldn't think why. People sat around listening and the blank expressions on their faces made me wonder if none of them understood his words either. I wanted to ask Jobi who he was and what he was saying, but somehow the words wouldn't come. So I sat and watched. Slowly it dawned on me that this man reminded me of the *ngan-*

ga who had carried off the dead body of the green mamba I had caught at Sheko Farm; the same man who had come and stared at me when Robert and I were by the crested cranes' pen. But this was miles from home. Surely it couldn't be the same man? Maybe he had a brother who looked like him? I decided he was certainly a *nganga*, and wondered if all witch-doctors looked the same.

The man took no notice of us at first, but suddenly paused in his monologue, pointing a stick directly at me. "I see you!" he announced. "You are welcome here." He gestured to Alistair, tossed his head and said, "This one is lost. Take him back to his own people."

Jobi took that as his cue to usher us out of the compound. A few moments later we heard the Land Rover beep a call for us to return. As we walked between the compounds, I told Jobi that the man looked like someone I'd seen before, and asked who he was and what he had been talking about.

"He is *nganga*. He was talking to the spirits," was all Jobi would say.

"Could he be the same man I saw at Sheko Farm, near Lusaka?"

"Maybe." He was obviously uncomfortable talking about the man, so I dropped it.

I wondered how you were supposed to learn about *ngangas*, spirits and the like if you weren't allowed to ask questions about them. I had heard a bit about witch-doctors and spirits from Robert and Gilbert, but this was only the second one I had seen and known what he was. The image of him sitting, speaking strange words that everyone listened to but nobody understood stuck in my mind for a long time.

When we got back to the centre, we were delighted to

Gordon, me and Alistair with the young Grevy's zebras.

discover a pair of young zebra in a corral behind the house. They were remarkably tame and friendly, coming over to investigate as soon as we pushed our hands through the railings. They accepted our pats without shying away. I learned later that they were being hand-reared because a lion had killed their mothers. They could have been left to run with the herd, but since they had been only days old at the time, they would probably have starved. Now eight months old, they were almost half-grown. Gerry's son, Gordon, said they were tame enough to ride. Hearing this, I was desperate to try, but it was getting dark and would have to wait for another opportunity.

We were about to turn away from the pen, when the witch-doctor we had seen earlier appeared out of the bushes. He stared at me with gimlet eyes for a minute, then grunted and turned away. He offered no greeting and no explanation of why he came, or what he wanted, but he clearly came to take a look at me. I resolved to ask more about this enigmatic man.

THE FOLLOWING MORNING, Jobi, Gordon and I, with another ranger called Membo, set off to look for elephants while

Gerry took Dad and Alistair with him while he sorted out a problem with a leopard that villagers complained was attacking their
cattle. It was going to be a great adventure. We were going to
camp out in the park overnight. The Land Rover was loaded up
with our bedding rolls and a box of catering essentials. The
rangers checked the water and spare fuel tanks, clipped a rifle into
the vehicle's gun rack – and we were off.

It took all morning to find the herd of elephants the rangers
wanted to look at. The rangers were both good trackers and knew
the animals' habits well, so we were never going to be disappointed. The first herd was quite small, numbering only about ten cows
and calves. We saw several solitary bulls, big animals with impressive tusks that turned to face us as we passed, scenting the air with
their trunks while their huge ears flapped to keep the flies off, and
to cool them in the heat of the day. We also saw lots of other animals. The two rangers told us their names and described their
habits. Living in the game park, Gordon was already familiar with
many of these animals from trips out with his father, but to me
they were all exciting and exotic, even the dainty duiker, the smallest of the antelopes. I also loved the colourful birds. When I
remarked on this, Jobi told me I should wait for morning to
appreciate the birds as then they would all sing together.

By late afternoon, we stopped. The rangers wanted to make
camp before it was dark. They chose an open glade several hundred yards from a small stream, with a good stand of thorny bushes nearby. Normally they camped out in the open with a small fire,
but with us two boys along they had been instructed to construct
a *boma*. They set about the thorn bushes with their machetes,
hacking off branches and building them into a tangled prickly bar-
ricade around the Land Rover, leaving space enough for a fire and

for the four of us to stretch out our bed rolls. The fence should deter prowling predators long enough for the two rangers to take action and chase them away. If anything hostile came visiting during the night, Gordon and I were to climb into the Land Rover.

With our *boma* complete, we collected firewood, and bundles of long grass to make our beds more comfortable.

During the afternoon, Membo had used a slingshot to kill two Guinea fowl. It was an impressive skill that I insisted he teach me. Whirling the thing round my head with a small stone in the leather pouch, I tried and tried, but was remarkably unsuccessful at launching the pebble in the direction I intended, let alone hitting anything. Gordon snorted in disgust and produced a catapult from his back pocket. He launched stone after stone in quick succession at a nearby tree, hitting it every time. Membo wasn't impressed and challenged him to hit a tree twice the distance away. His stone never even reached the target.

Membo loaded his slingshot, flicked it once round his head and launched a stone. Before it found its mark, he had another one in the air and was whirling a third around his head as the first stone hit the remote tree. All three hit unerringly. He rolled his slingshot, stuffed it in his pocket and walked off, saying nothing. Gordon looked sheepish. I felt more determined than ever to learn how to use a slingshot.

For supper that night we ate the Guinea fowl roasted over open coals and *sadza* the rangers had brought with us. Nothing ever tasted so good as we sat round the fire, watching small showers of sparks rise into the clear night air, merging with the stars until they winked into oblivion. Membo told me the stars were the camp fires of the ancestors. They were looking down from the spirit world to see that we kept the world as they had left it. Jobi snorted and said they were just stars. He was a Christian and didn't believe in ancestors, except in the abstract. To him they were just people who had once lived. I liked Membo's version better.

That was when I chose to ask about the witch-doctor, hoping Jobi would explain. Whatever I expected, I was disappointed as Jobi simply said he was a bad man, and I should not mix with people like him. He messed around with spirits and did not respect Jesus. While I'd heard similar things from the nuns at school, they'd never shown any of the passion Jobi did, and it was clear he really did believe all this stuff about spirits. I was more inclined to listen to Jobi and Membo than the nuns, but was still curious to know more about the *nganga*.

After supper, we lay on our beds and stared up at the stars until the crescent moon crept over the horizon, spreading a thin silvery sheen over the countryside. We listened to the churring of nightjars and the rustling of small nocturnal animals in the grass. From some distance away came a dull roaring sound. It was very familiar, yet I had no idea what made the noise. That sound was something elemental that had been with me all my life, but I didn't know what it was. When I asked Jobi, he said "Lions", and a string of connections from my earliest years fell into place.

In Scotland, we had lived about half a mile from Edinburgh zoo. From my earliest days, Mum took me around the zoo in my pram. We always stopped in front of the lion cage. As I got older and could walk, it was one of my favourite places to stop. I would stare at the huge golden cats, lazing on a pile of logs, or patrolling the perimeter fence of their enclosure. Most of the time they were lazy and did little, and none ever made a sound, but they stopped patrolling occasionally and stared back at us with mesmerising yellow eyes. From home we could hear them roaring at night, when lions are most active. The sound embedded itself in my consciousness without my ever knowing what it was.

Now I knew.

Membo said the lions were telling tales to the ancestors, which they could only do properly at night when all the other noisy beasts of the world were asleep. Jobi immediately said it was indigestion and that he groaned like this if his wife produced food he didn't like. This exchange made us laugh, and I began to realise that, as with their explanations of the stars, there was a continual banter between Jobi and Membo based on their differing beliefs. But they were, nevertheless, the very best of friends.

Other sounds intruded: the yapping of jackals, the hooting laugh of a hyena, and a variety of hoots and whistles from night birds in the nearby trees. But nothing tried to invade our *boma*. As the fire died down to red coals, sleep crept over me, laden with tangled dreams of lions talking to ethereal ancestors, elephants trumpeting as they screamed out messages across the open bush, hyenas laughing because they found everything so funny, and giraffes striding gracefully across the open countryside, looking down on all the other beasts with their huge, limpid eyes.

I was brought back to the real world by a cacophony of hoots, shrieks and whistles. The fire smouldered in a pile of warm ash. The air was cool, the moon had set, and the stars no longer glittered so brightly, fading as they were re-absorbed into their black sea by the approaching dawn. Dawn and dusk come rapidly in these latitudes, and this in-between time lasts for only about twenty minutes.

Even so, the morning is a time when the calm of the night is shattered by noise, even in the most remote, apparently empty bush places. Every creature in creation wants to advertise its presence, to scream, whistle, hoot or roar at the new day. Birds, almost unnoticed by their calls during the day, fill the air with music, shrieks and squawks. Small sunbirds twitter in the acacia branches, hornbills honk, yellow weaver birds chitter and squabble, and others whistle and chirrup until the sun casts its first golden glow across the landscape. Then everything quietens down as they all go about their daily business, seeking water and food, collecting grass and twigs to repair nests or to build new ones or, in the case of owls and nightjars, settling down to sleep after their night's hunting.

Membo soon coaxed our fire awake with dry grass and twigs to boil a kettle for tea. The hot liquid was welcome in the cool morning air, and helped us swallow our breakfast of stodgy *sadza*, left over from the previous night's supper. Jobi decided we needed more than that for breakfast and produced a paper-wrapped packet of bacon he had brought along. A metal plate laid over the fire served as a griddle and soon the aroma of sizzling bacon had all our mouths watering. I decided breakfast in the bush was the best, and I would have so much to tell Mum and Dad and Alistair when we got back to the centre.

We found elephants again that morning and spent a long time following them as they ambled through the bush with no sense of urgency, picking up tufts of grass and kicking the soil off their roots, stripping small branches from bushes and trees as they went, and rumbling gently to one another. We saw how the older cows moved to shield their *totos*, always keeping them close, and we watched how the younger animals played games, pushing and shoving, and slapping one another with their trunks. When they crossed a small river, the herd paused to drink and to play. The elder ones drew up water in their trunks, spraying it over their backs and over each other, while the youngsters rolled and frolicked in the shallow water, always surrounded and watched by adults.

The rangers knew that two of the cows in this herd were due to give birth and they had been particularly keen to check if they had, but we could see no newborns, so they'd have to wait a few more days. We followed slowly and watched the herd anyway for several hours.

At the river, Jobi pointed out three crocodiles on the far bank and we watched them for a while, hoping they might slide into the water. But they just lay inert like knobbly logs. Perhaps they knew they were no match for a whole herd of elephants. Jobi said they would wait for easier prey, when gazelle or wildebeest came in their dozens to drink. Then they would get lunch. Before that they would slide into the water and submerge, ready to attack with surprise when the grazers bent down to drink, grabbing them by the throat and pulling them into the river to drown. Until the herds came, they would simply bask in the sun, absorbing its warmth.

We arrived back at the ranger station just before sunset, having made a huge circular loop through the northern part of the park. While Jobi and Membo were putting the rifle back in its cabinet, another Land Rover, muddy and dented, arrived. It was Gerry, Dad and my brother, together with another African ranger. They hadn't intended to stay out overnight, but the discussions about the leopard had taken longer than they expected – and then there had been an incident with a hippo down on the Kafue River.

When it became clear they would be staying, the chief of the village with the leopard problem cleared a hut for them while Gerry went into the bush and shot a buck as a gift to the villagers. It also ensured they got fresh meat for supper, which was a relief to Alistair because he didn't like *posho,* which was all the villagers had to offer.

This morning they had gone to the river to find out about the hippo, which had stampeded through a small fishing village, smashing several of the fishermen's huts and crushing a child. The fishermen had complained before about a rogue hippo in the area, but so far nobody had been able to identify precisely which animal was responsible. This time one of the villagers had managed to stab it with a spear. The shaft of the spear had broken off but the head was still stuck in the animal's shoulder when it returned to the river.

Down at the river it was not too difficult to identify the rogue animal. She was standing alone on the riverbank, munching leaves, while the rest of the herd was wallowing in the shallow water. Unfortunately she was on the far bank, just downstream of the fishermen's huts. Gerry was unwilling to shoot across the river without knowing what lay beyond, so they borrowed a fisherman's dug-out canoe and set off across the river about two hundred yards upstream of the hippo with two fishermen paddling. Luck was against them. By the time they got across, the hippo had ambled into the water and submerged. She showed nothing more than ears, eyes and nostrils above the brown water and so was indistinguishable from all the others in the herd.

Inevitably the fishermen wanted to talk about the incident, and took the visitors on a tour of the destruction the animal had caused. They exhibited the broken spear shaft and re-enacted the way it got broken with great drama. Everyone made it plain that they wanted the animal shot. The fishermen had lived for years with hippos and crocodiles in their river without any trouble. They left the animals alone, and the animals ignored them. But an evil spirit had taken possession of this particular beast, which was now terrorising them. The few crops they grew had been flattened and eaten. Now their houses had been flattened, and one of their children had been trampled to death. The hippo had to go.

The talking went on and on until late afternoon, while the hippos wallowed in the river, showing no sign of coming out. Eventually Gerry said they'd have to get it later. He left his ranger in the village armed with a rifle in case it came out before dusk. Meanwhile he, Dad and Alistair would go back to the park centre, and return after dark, when the hippos should emerge from the river to graze. He would hunt the offending beast by spotlight.

Once again they set off across the river in the dug-out canoe. They hadn't gone far when there was a tremendous commotion in the river behind them. The water churned and a huge brown form surged out of the water, upended the canoe, and tipped everyone into the shallows. It then proceeded to crush the canoe, using its massive weight and huge tusked jaws to splinter the brittle wood.

Everyone managed to scramble safely ashore and retreat to higher ground, where the Land Rover was parked. Unfortunately Gerry's rifle had been soaked in the commotion, so he was unable to shoot immediately. Standing behind the Land Rover, he was stripping it down to clean and reload when the hippo decided to attack the vehicle. Mouth gaping wide, it smashed into the Land Rover with its tusks, pushing it bodily down the bank into a muddy gully as if it weighed no more than an empty dustbin. By the time it came to rest, the animal's fury had subsided and it just stood and stared myopically at the tipped-up vehicle.

As soon as Gerry had dried and reloaded the rifle, he skipped across to the far side of the gully so he could see the hippo face on, and put three rapid shots into its brain. The hippo subsided in a heap and everyone relaxed. The broken-off spear head was still stuck firmly in its shoulder.

Seeing the commotion on the river bank, other fishermen soon came across in their canoes. With ropes from the back of the Land Rover, they helped haul the battered vehicle out of the gully and back onto dry land, loudly thanking and praising Gerry for having killed the monster. He told them they could have the carcass. Its meat would keep their little community fed for weeks and, once it had been cut into strips and smoked, they would have plenty of *biltong* to sell in the markets. This would be their compensation for the damage the hippo had done to their village.

Despite all these dramatic tales of hippos and crocodiles, the following day Dad borrowed one of the game park's Land Rovers and took us to the Kafue River to swim. Although Alistair had learned to swim in Scotland, I had not, so he and Mum climbed into the water and swam up and down, staying in the shallow water within about twenty feet of the bank. Dad and I sat on the bank above them watching carefully, Dad with a loaded rifle across his knees in case a crocodile should take an undue interest.

After a while we changed places. Dad took me into the water and began by teaching me how to float. At first I kept sinking and tried to kick my way back to the surface.

"Don't thrash about so much, you'll attract the crocodiles," Dad said.

But it was no use. I didn't know how else to keep myself at the surface. I carried on thrashing until there was an almighty bang. That stopped me and I stood up, to find my mother standing above us on the bank, the rifle held tightly to her shoulder, aiming at something in the river not far beyond me.

Dad and I scrambled to the bank and out of the water in time to see the water behind us swirl and a scaly tail break the surface. Moments later there was a wild thrashing as two more crocs turned on the one Mum had shot, and we watched in horror. There would be no point in staying here now, hoping to swim when they all went away. We'd have to try again somewhere else, another day.

So ended my first swimming lesson.

Two days later, when we were returning to Lusaka, we stopped by the ferry and swam again. That area was so busy with boats and other activity that the crocodiles stayed well clear, and there was a small beach beside the ferry landing where it was safe to swim. An excited crowd of naked children joined us. They made swimming look easy. This was all the encouragement I needed, and by emulating them, I soon managed to stay afloat and found the strokes came easily.

The next time we went swimming in Lusaka, I leapt in the deep end without hesitation. It was fun, but somehow not as much fun in the clean clear water of the pool as it had been with the merry crowd at the Kafue ferry. Apart from anything else, there were almost no African children at the swimming pool and the European kids didn't seem to have the same zest for fun. Some of their parents also frowned on my bringing Robert, Gilbert and Nasouma with me to swim. I didn't think it was right for the pool to be only for officers' families, but Mum said that was the rule, so that was how it had to be. She didn't make the rules, she added when I gave her a disappointed look.

11 ~ A time of celebration

LISTENING TO OUR CRACKLING, whistling short-wave radio, we heard the news that King George had died, but it meant little to me. All the European adults were sad and walked around with long faces. My African friends and I couldn't understand what all the fuss was about: he had only gone to be an ancestor, and that was a normal enough thing. When I made the mistake of saying this at school, Sister Monica smacked me round the head for being disrespectful and made me stand in a corner for an hour. It didn't bother me as it got me out of the incessant chanting and I spent the time watching a small translucent gecko catching flies, somehow hanging on despite the smooth surface of the whitewashed wall.

Sister Monica somehow got word about what I'd said back to my father. That evening, I got a lecture on being properly respectful. I told Dad the nuns were horrid and didn't like the King anyway. He explained that the sisters looked at things a little differently and I ought to learn to understand that. There might be nothing wrong with what I'd said, but I had offended them by saying it. I needed to make allowances for other people's views.

"You mean like Jobi and Membo?" I asked, for he too had heard their banter.

"Exactly. They hold different views, but they leave each other space to believe what they choose."

"So why did Sister Monica call me a little heathen and hit me? She said I ought to be a good Christian and not pay attention to all this 'super-sticky' stuff the Africans say." To me, still feeling aggrieved, that didn't sound much like respecting other people's views.

"She's what we call Catholic, and they take a more rigid view of things," he explained. "We've been brought up with the *kirk* in Scotland, and our way is simpler. But it's only like looking at the same thing through different windows. You need to learn about the nuns' ways, but not necessarily adopt them. When you're older, and you know more, you can choose."

That sounded fair enough, so I dropped the matter, but I still didn't like the nuns. Except Sister Bernadette.

BY THE TIME my birthday came round in April 1953, the camp was abuzz with the news that the Army was putting on a tattoo to mark the coronation in two months' time. Large formations of soldiers seemed to be always on the parade ground, marching up and down, wheeling and stamping, trying to wear out the grass. Even when they weren't in dress uniform, the *askaris* had a striking presence, and their drill was crisp and well-timed. A regiment of Guards would have been proud of their formations.

In the afternoons when we came back from school, my friends and I used to watch them from a perch on a wall at the edge of the parade ground, beneath a pair of rusting anti-aircraft guns left over from the war. One afternoon a group of the soldiers' wives gathered at the edge of the parade ground. When the marching ceased, they moved forward to dance in a troop, singing and clapping as they moved. They seemed to flow over the open space, a loose fluid wave of colour and rhythm, a bright flood contrasting with the crisp movements of the *askaris*.

As we watched, Gilbert remarked that his mother was among them. A few moments later, Robert spotted Ruth. My mother was nowhere to be seen. Nor were any of the other white wives, although one or two had been watching earlier from the other side of the parade ground, while the *askaris* were marching. I felt slightly disappointed.

Eventually the practice ended and the field was left empty, a vast green space of open ground, surrounded by white painted rocks, shady, scarlet-flowered flame trees and blue-crowned jacarandas.

We wandered homewards to make our daily inspection of the crested cranes. This afternoon all four of them danced for us, dipping their heads, spreading their wings and strutting about in exaggerated postures. Even the birds seemed to be celebrating. We three boys felt left out.

"We should do something ourselves for the coronation," I said to nobody in particular.

"What could we do?" Robert asked.

"Dance," I said, remembering how we had joined the troops that first New Year, when they came around to salute their European officers.

"But there are only three of us," Gilbert said.

"There are over fifty in our class at school, and most of them are Army kids."

And so an idea was born.

At school a few days later, others eagerly agreed to join our dance and we began working out formations and movements in the playground during the morning break. By the end of the week, almost every child in the school wanted to be involved, even the village kids who did not come from Army families.

The nuns weren't impressed. They didn't approve and put a stop to our preparations in the playground, saying it was disrespectful. It didn't stop small groups trying, but Sister Esmeralda was almost incandescent in her fury. She confined us all to our classrooms and our mid-morning break disappeared.

This caused grumbles and resentment. One minute they told us off for being disrespectful when the King died. The next, they were telling us off for doing something like everyone else to celebrate the new Queen's coronation. Where was the sense in that?

That afternoon the bus back to the barracks was more crowded than usual as children from the surrounding villages came with us. Behind the armoury, near where we got off the bus, was a clear patch of ground where we often played football. It would do for practising our songs and dancing. A few *askaris* and their wives came to see what all the noise was about. They soon began cheering and encouraging us once they understood what we were doing.

It was another week before the hierarchy took any notice of us. Then a young National Service officer was sent to find out what we were doing. He told us the nuns at the mission school had complained about the behaviour of the Army children. He had been instructed to visit the school to see what the problem was. After listening to our explanation, he watched our dancing for a few minutes, and left smiling.

There was no sign of the officer when we boarded the bus the following morning, but when we arrived at school, an Army Land

Rover was already parked there. The officer was in conference with Sister Esmeralda. The two of them emerged from her office to watch as we disembarked and lined up in our form groups before class. At ten o'clock, we were surprised to be allowed out for fifteen minutes for mid-morning break, having been denied it all the previous week. Nobody said anything about not singing and dancing, so we did. The nuns glared at us from the shade of the veranda.

When we got off the bus that afternoon, the officer was waiting for us. He watched for a while before coming over to talk to us. He'd understood what we were doing, but said the tattoo was already organised and planned and there wasn't a slot for us to perform as part of it.

"Why not?" I demanded.

"Well, er... there just isn't. It's all very precisely timed, and... er... there isn't time for anything else." He seemed slightly confused that I should presume to ask such a question.

"But if our mothers are going to dance to celebrate the Queen, why can't we?" I said.

"Because, er... it doesn't fit the plan," he finally spluttered, clearly put out by my impertinence.

"Must be a rotten plan if it can't be changed," I said. "My Dad says you always have to plan for unexpected contingencies."

He was clearly fed up with this cheeky white brat answering back, so he demanded, "So who's your dad if he knows so much about everything, then?"

"Major Mathie, the two IC."

We all saw his Adam's apple jerk up and down his throat as he swallowed. That was clearly not what he expected to hear.

"Well I didn't make the plan," he muttered. Without further

comment, he turned and marched stiffly in the direction of the station admin offices.

That evening Dad quizzed me about what we had been doing. After I had explained, he even went out to the cook's quarters, to talk to Robert. He had smiled when I told him about my conversation with the young officer, but said that if I was cheeky like that again our plan would definitely go no further. As it was, he saw no reason why, if our little dance troop was good enough, we shouldn't participate in the tattoo. He would discuss the idea with the CO and the major who was running the event.

Two days later, when we got off the school bus, the young officer was waiting for us again. He was not alone this time. Beside him was one of the company commanders, Major Bunn. The lieutenant introduced him as the officer in command of the tattoo, and he'd come to see our performance. By this time, we were quite well organised, and having an official audience made everyone perform to their best.

Since it had been the idea of Robert, Gilbert and me in the first place, the rest of the kids had somehow always pushed us to the front of the display. This time when we started, Gilbert and I stepped slightly backwards to merge with the first line, leaving Robert in front to lead us. His dad always led the formation when the troops danced, so we felt he should lead ours. By the time we finished our routine, we had attracted a bigger audience of Army wives and officers, including my Dad. They melted away when we finished, but Major Bunn and the lieutenant waited to talk to us.

"That was pretty good. So we'll make a slot to include you in the tattoo, but you'll have to limit your routine to six minutes. Can you do that?"

"Yes!" cried sixty voices in unison.

Some months later, when I had accompanied the soldiers into the bush on one of their exercises in preparation for deployment to Malaya, Major Bunn told me it was the unity and enthusiasm of our response that day which convinced him he'd made the right decision.

One of our gang was a boy called Dege Masolele. He desperately wanted to be part of the enterprise, but couldn't dance because he had a deformed foot. He could, however, beat a drum, so he became our drummer, setting the rhythm and tempo of the dance. Now he also became the time-keeper. Beside him now sat a large borrowed alarm clock. As six minutes neared, he changed the beat to tell us we were getting to the end. We had to adapt the routine slightly and cut out a bit of the singing, but it worked and we made our routine fit our allocated time.

We had ideas for fancy costumes but in the end, it became too complicated, too expensive – and we ran out of time to make them. So we wore our school uniforms: white shirts and green shorts for the boys and green skirts for the girls.

The coronation tattoo took place on Friday 5 June, three days after Queen Elizabeth was crowned in London. All the local dignitaries were there, including various foreign delegates and a gathering of the tribal chiefs. The Speaker of the Representative Council, who acted as governor of the protectorate, as Northern Rhodesia was then, would take the salute from a white dais.

Rows of chairs and benches had been set out around the perimeter of the parade ground, with flags on poles and bunting hung between the trees, whose trunks were whitewashed to a height of precisely three feet. The large rocks that surrounded the parade ground had been freshly whitewashed, along with hundreds of others alongside all the roads in the camp. Even the stones which lined the drive in our garden received the same treatment, together with the front wall of the house. If it didn't move, it got painted in the effort to spruce everything up. The old anti-aircraft guns were cleaned by the armourers and given a coat of smart green camouflage paint. The *pièce de résistance* of the whole show was a large fort. Constructed of wood, it looked like something out of a cowboy film and was situated next to where the band would be playing for most of the event. This fort was to be the scene of a battle enactment, with lots of bangs, smoke, and troops charging about letting off flares. Painted a dull grey, it looked quite imposing on the edge of the empty field.

The day of the tattoo found the parade ground surrounded by people in party mood. The band played, *askaris* marched in quick and slow time, their long ranks wheeling past the dais where the Governor stood with the commanding officer to accept the salutes. Army fitness instructors followed up with displays of gymnastics before a small formation of *askaris* returned for a complicated marching display.

In the middle of this, a swarm of wild bees flew across the parade ground and settled on the top of the fort. Some landed among the musicians, causing instant panic from one side of the band. Several musicians dropped their instruments and began slapping one another to brush off the stinging invaders.

Moments later, men waiting for the big set piece battle erupted from the fort and ran off screaming. Soldiers broke from their formations at the side of the ground and brought fire buckets, dowsing the afflicted bandsmen. The station fire truck arrived, its hose spouting, soaking more of the band than necessary. Through all this pandemonium, a few stalwart musicians played on.

Eventually a man with a skep captured the swarm and the

band sorted itself out. Some musicians headed off to the station medical centre for treatment, leaving a much-reduced band to play out the marching *askaris* routine.

And then it was our turn. We had already advanced onto the open ground, stamping in unison with Dege's lone drumbeat, but not yet singing. We were waiting for a signal from our drummer. When his rhythm changed, we knew we had six minutes. He had mastered the art of setting the borrowed alarm clock and as he changed the beat we dimly heard the ringing of its bell over the excited voices of those around us.

As we retired from the field, a swaying, singing crocodile of army wives sashayed onto the open ground. They had no accompaniment, but needed none. Their voices singing counterpoint to a chanter, filled the afternoon air, ululations punctuating their song. We were wondering how long they were going to continue when some of the troops returned. They had changed into their traditional warrior costumes – basically a short antelope-skin kilt, bunches of cow tails round their ankles and arms, a few feathers stuck in their hair, a shield and a spear. Their voices swelled as they had each year at Christmas and New Year, their feet stamping out a powerful rhythm on the hard ground. This time they had a drummer, and as the broad front of warriors advanced, it was too much for the women. Their voices diminished to nothing as they melted away into the crowd of watchers.

As before, Gideon, our cook, was at the front. It gave me an intense feeling of pride to realise that the man leading this dramatic and impressive band of warriors was my friend, just as his son, who had led our children's dance, was also my friend. I felt part of something timeless yet eternal.

Their dance this time was not honorific, for they were singing

The 2nd Northern Rhodesia Regiment marching onto the parade ground for the Coronation Parade with the band on the right and the fort in the background. My father is the nearest of the three officers leading the troops.

fighting songs as their company advanced on the fort. Bangs went off, clods of earth rose from the ground among the dancers as their formation attacked the fort, and some of the men fell spectacularly on the field. As the smoke cleared, a company of *askaris* in uniform emerged from the fort and, with lots more bangs and a few more dramatic falls, drove the warriors away.

The marching soldiers came back to Beat Retreat and perform the final ceremonial march-past in long straight ranks. They must have been tired after such an energetic afternoon, but they still performed well, their ranks straight as guardsmen at the Trooping of the Colour. As the last troops left the parade ground to march back to their barracks, they began singing songs of praise. We could hear their voices all the way back to the lines.

Then we all went home.

12 ~ Honoured

WHEN WE GOT HOME that evening, Dad said he had enjoyed our performance and thought we'd done a good job. He also said he wanted Robert, Gilbert and me, all scrubbed clean, in our school uniforms and on parade outside our front door at ten to eleven the next morning. He wouldn't explain why, but told me the other two already knew. To change the subject, he talked about the chaos the bees had caused. One of the bandsmen had received more than fifty stings and was still being treated.

The following morning, Mum looked me over, straightened my school uniform, smoothed my hair and ushered me out the front door to where Robert and Gilbert were waiting. So was a smart army staff car. We climbed into the back seat, while Dad sat in front with the driver.

"Where are we going?" I asked, as the car started to move.

"Government House," Dad said over his shoulder.

It was only a few miles, through the centre of town, and we all sat silent and awed, feeling important. At Government House, a uniformed footman opened the car door and ushered us inside the building. We followed Dad to a grand room brightly lit, with a line of whirring fans hanging from the ceiling. A crowd of about twenty adults, all dressed in their finest, murmured quietly to one another and, many looking uncomfortable, waited for something to happen.

After a few minutes, the hushed conversation ceased when the Governor appeared, resplendent in the uniform he had worn the day before, with gold tassels dangling from his shoulder. A uniformed attendant stood behind him, holding his feathered hat. Several other attendants stood to one side holding trays. The only thing that seemed to be missing was the cocktails. But that was not why we were there.

One at a time, people were called forward to stand in front of the Governor. From the back of the room, we couldn't hear what he said to them, but he pinned something on each one's chest. After a brief handshake, they left through a door at the side of the room.

Ten or more people had been called when an official came and took Robert, Gilbert and me forward to meet the Governor together. He told us he was very impressed by our performance at the tattoo and, as the three boys responsible for organising it, he was awarding each of us a Coronation Medal.

"But everybody in our class did it," Gilbert said.

"I know, but you three thought up the idea and made it happen. You were the leaders. This award is for your leadership," the Governor replied, and he pinned a medal on each of our shirts, just above the pocket.

As we walked towards the side door, I caught sight of Mum, together with Ruth and Gideon, all dressed up and standing among a crowd at the side of the room, grinning. I wanted to rush over and show her the medal, but the man guiding us said we'd see our families outside in the garden. So we did, and Gilbert's parents were there too. While we sipped at lemon squash in large glasses with ice cubes tinkling in them, Mum told me that she'd followed behind the staff car in our battered old Ford, and brought the others with her.

Thinking about this, years later, I understood why the people who worked for her were always so willing. They loved her, and would do anything she asked. Mum knew how proud Ruth and Gideon Chilomo and Samala and Moses Chileshe were that their boys had been chosen to receive this medal. They, like any other parents, deserved the joy of seeing the presentation. They would never normally go anywhere near Government House, let alone attend a formal event. So she brought them along and would take no argument from the doorman who tried to refuse them entry.

In its own quiet way, this was pure leadership and it was she who deserved the medal for leadership, not me. I've always been proud of her for doing that.

My Coronation Medal.

13 ~ A burst radiator and zebra riding

ON MONDAY MORNING, IT was back to school. Of course the place was abuzz with talk about the coronation, the tattoo and our performance. We brought our medals to show our classmates, recognising we wouldn't have received them without everyone's participation. The nuns looked on disapprovingly, and told us to put them away before class.

At break time, a new dance started, re-enacting the tattoo, in particular the bees' invasion. Although this had been painful, even dangerous for the bandsmen, the event had had its funny side too. With the innocence of childhood, we exploited this to the maximum. The nuns were not amused. We all noticed the discipline at school was tighter than ever that week and the hands that slapped us for misdemeanours struck with more force than usual.

Before long, the summer term ended and we had six weeks free from the nuns' censorious domination. The mood on the bus going home after our last day was buoyant. Nobody minded when the bus got a puncture and we all had to disembark and wait by the roadside while the driver changed the wheel. As chance would have it, this happened close to a local landmark in the form of a split *kopje*. Two huge rock outcrops, one either side of the road, dominated the rolling countryside here. Legend had it that a man-eating leopard lived in these rocks, but nobody had ever made a confirmed sighting. Even so, it made an interesting topic for discussion while we stood around, and some of the more timid children tried to climb back into the bus in case the leopard came looking for an easy meal. The driver chased them out, so we milled about in the bush beside the road until he was done.

Always on the lookout for anything interesting in the bush, I caught a *kalilombe*, or chameleon, and brought it onto the bus when we re-embarked. Some of the children from more traditional families were scared of chameleons, saying they were a devil's totem, and screaming if I went anywhere near them. The bus driver was also scared of it. He leapt from his seat and refused to get back in and drive until I released the creature. He didn't realise I'd caught two, and had managed to keep the other one hidden until the bus had almost reached the barracks gate. When he did realise, he slammed on the brakes, leapt from his seat, and ran into the guard house by the gate. The guard sergeant came out a few minutes later and told us the bus would be going no further. We'd have to disembark and walk the rest of the way. It was only about half a mile to the lines where most of the children lived, so this was no problem. It was a bit further for Robert and me, but there was a shortcut across a patch of rough ground, so we took that. I released the second *kalilombe* in a shrub, hoping it wouldn't be too lonely without the mate we'd left up the road, and wondering if their spirits could communicate over such a distance.

That summer we went to the Kafue Game Park again. This time we stayed longer as our visit had an extra purpose: Dad was

on a recruiting drive for the Army. As second in command of the
Northern Rhodesia Regiment, it was one of his responsibilities to
ensure a steady flow of new recruits to replace the soldiers who
had served their enlistment and were retiring. Many of his best
soldiers came from the tribes that lived beyond the Kafue River, so
he had decided to enlist the help of the game ranger in recruiting
new men. Gerry Taylor knew the tribes well and could advise on
which villages to approach.

This time the road to Mumbwa and beyond had recently been
graded, which enabled fast, smooth driving and we were able to
average forty miles an hour. We got no punctures this time, but the
trip was not without its drama. Five miles after crossing the Kafue
River, the inside of the car filled with a cloud of smelly steam.
Bringing the car to a standstill, miles from anywhere, Dad said he
thought a radiator hose had burst. He lifted the bonnet flaps to
reveal the usually pristine engine, now covered in drying dusty
water stains and smelling like a rusty sewage works. The radiator
hoses were intact – the radiator itself had burst.

There were no magic products for sealing radiators in those
days. Mending it would require a soldering iron and a trip to a
workshop. But we still had about forty miles to go and there were
no mechanics out here on this bush road.

Normally, wherever you stop in Africa, even in the most isolated palces, someone will appear, apparently from nowhere, to
stand and stare at you. Even if you can't go yourself, this at least
offers the opportunity of sending someone to bring help. But on
this occasion there was nobody. We were on our own.

By peering at it from every angle, and using the make-up mirror from Mum's handbag, Dad identified the problem as a small
hole near the top, on the left hand side of the radiator. He thought

a stone flicked up off the road had probably caused it. It took a good fifteen minutes to cool down enough to touch. Dad used the can of water we carried to refill the radiator. It swallowed half the can before water started pouring out of the hole he had found. This didn't augur well. The hole would have to be plugged if we were to go any further.

Desperate situations call for desperate measures and, after rootling about in the boot among the supplies she had brought with us, Mum produced a large can of mustard powder and a bag of flour. Dad opted for the mustard and just a little flour, mixing this to a thin slurry with a little of the remaining water. As soon as he had poured this into the top of the radiator and added the rest of the water, Mum started the engine. Dad closed the bonnet and we set off immediately. We kept up a steady thirty miles per hour, anxiously watching the temperature gauge on the dashboard.

We may have done about fifteen or twenty miles before the temperature became too hot and Dad said we'd better stop before the engine seized up. Then we sat for half an hour while the engine cooled down again. Removing the filler cap revealed no water in the header tank, so in went the last of the water from the can, together with more mustard and flour slurry. We had to tip in drinking water as well before the header tank showed any sign of water, and again we set off at a steady pace.

Five miles before our destination, the temperature gauge reached its top limit. Once more we stopped; once more we sat and waited for the engine to cool. When it had reached an acceptable level, the last of our drinking water went into the radiator, followed by the flask of tea, which fortunately nobody had thought to drink earlier. But even with this contribution, the level was still too low. Two large bottles of gin that Mum had been

We boys had to stand on the front bumper and pee into the radiator.

intending to give to Gerry's wife followed the tea into the header tank and it was still not enough. As a final solution, Dad, Alistair and I each had to stand on the front bumper and pee into the radiator. This finally brought the fluid up to a visible level.

Dad hastily replaced the radiator cap, closed the bonnet flaps and drove on. We finally arrived at the game park centre just as the temperature needle again reached its maximum. Gerry and his wife were most amused by our escapade, not in the least dismayed that the gin had ended up in our radiator, and promised that their mechanic would start repairs in the morning.

THE ZEBRAS THAT HAD been in the pen behind the house last time we visited were still here, just as friendly, and now much bigger. They were also willing to be ridden, so Gordon and I spent a lot of time climbing on their backs and riding round the paddock. We had neither saddles nor bridles, and steered by pushing the side of the zebra's neck with one hand while holding onto a tuft of mane with the other. Occasionally they'd go where we wanted.

One evening after Gordon and I had been out playing with the zebras, we decided to go and find out what our parents were doing. There was a long corridor from the back door by the cookhouse that led into the main part of the house. This had a concrete floor painted cardinal red and polished to a deep shine. The passage was about forty feet long with storeroom doorways on one side. The other end of the passage emerged into the main living area of the house. We thought it would be great fun to take the zebras in there and say hello.

Zebras are normally sure-footed, but the polished floor was very slippery. Coming in quite fast, their unshod hooves skidded on the shiny surface and splayed out until the wall on each side stopped them. We shuffled along the corridor, one behind the other, with the zebras' legs braced against the passage walls until we erupted into the living quarters.

We thought it was very funny, but our parents weren't amused at two stripy animals ridden by giggling lunatics, charging round their living room. After they'd chased the animals out, they made us clean up the piles of dung the zebras had dropped in their excitement, and then get down on hands and knees and re-polish the scuffed corridor floor. From then on, the back door remained firmly closed.

A couple of army wagons arrived a few days later. Dad left Mum and me at the centre and went off with Alistair and Gerry on his recruitment tour. They came back three days later, having sent one lorry with thirty men in it back to Lusaka. The next day, they set off in a different direction to try another area.

While they were away looking for recruits, Gordon and I went looking for leopards with Jobi and Membo. Since the rangers knew all the animals well, it didn't take long to locate a leopard, and I again marvelled at how well these two understood the park and the animals that lived in it. They could identify individual cats and knew where each had its usual range. At one point, it seemed that every time we passed a certain type of tree there was a leopard sleeping in the branches.

Most of the animals we saw were just lazing around, but Jobi showed us some real excitement down by the river. There was a place which antelope regularly used, both as a drinking spot and as a crossing point. Along the banks nearby, both crocodiles and leopards liked to lie in ambush as the pickings were easy.

Jobi parked his vehicle some distance from the river and from there we walked. He knew where the female leopard that lived nearby was most likely to be, as she had two cubs hidden in a den down by the river. The game trails, along which any antelope or other animals coming to drink would arrive, were easy to identify, so we steered clear of those. He led us to the foot of a large tree on a bluff overlooking the river. From there we could see the crossing and part of the animal track leading down to it on this side. Birds and exotic butterflies kept us occupied while we waited for animals; the damp mud of the river bank shimmered with colour as the butterflies settled on it.

When a small herd of about thirty gazelles arrived to drink, there was a sudden blur of golden movement, instantly followed by chaos among the group. In moments this resolved itself as all but one of the gazelles fled back up the bank. The unfortunate victim struggled and twitched in the jaws of a sleek spotted cat. Unconcerned, the leopard lay still beside the water, maintaining its grip on the gazelle's throat until all movement ceased. Then it stood up, adjusted its hold and dragged the carcass up the steep bank, towards some dense bushes that concealed its den. We caught a brief glimpse of the cubs, tumbling out to greet their mother before she dragged the carcass out of sight.

The whole business lasted less than two minutes, but engraved itself on my memory for a lifetime. I've seen other big cat kills since then, but none had the power and brutality, the terminal precision, and the absolute dominance of that one. That leopard was a highly efficient hunter, not given to wasted efforts.

For the rest of the week, Gordon and I accompanied the African rangers on their daily patrols. As well as watching animals, these duties included visits to some of the communities situated within the park to consult with their headmen and discuss problems where wild animals had invaded their small farms. We also spent time back at the rangers' centre, looking after and tending any sick animals that had been brought in and riding the two young zebras. The rangers had taken them out to join a wild herd a few months earlier, only for the zebras to turn around and bring themselves back to the centre, making it clear they liked the domestic life. They were no longer being fed, and relied on grazing around the station, but they never strayed far and always returned at night to stand beside the corral or close to the barn where they had grown up.

A number of other animals lived in pens and cages at the centre. They were either recovering from injury, or permanently resident because some deformity or old injury meant they would not survive in the wild. In conservation terms this was probably wasted effort, but it meant visitors could observe one or two of the lesser-known species. They were also good subject matter for Gerry's wife, who was a keen wildlife artist, to paint.

14 ~ Mansion and man-eater

WE MADE ANOTHER TRIP to Kafue that summer, this time in an army vehicle. Dad wanted to go further into the bush to visit Shiwa Ngandu. This was the home of an eccentric Englishman who had retired from the British Army after the end of the Great War and had come to Africa to make his fortune. Colonel Stewart Gore-Browne had started a farm in the north-western province of Northern Rhodesia, near the source of the great Congo River, and built himself an exotic mansion, up beyond Chinsali near Lake Ishiba Ng'andu.

Dad knew about his Army service and had heard of his reputation for getting on well with the local Bemba tribesmen. Some of the European community said Gore-Browne had 'gone native', but Dad felt he would be an ideal person to help recruit good men for the regiment. So he decided to go and find out.

With an army driver, the Land Rover laden with spares, and a trailer filled with a selection of things we hoped might be useful so far out in the bush, we headed north from the game park towards Kasempo. As soon as we left the game park, the roads began to deteriorate by the mile. We made much of the trip at little more

Shiwa Ngandu, the home of Colonel Stewart Gore-Browne.

than a fast trot, often in four-wheel drive. One night we camped out in the open, cutting thorn bushes to make a *boma* round the vehicle and tent, and cooking as before over an open fire. Dad had brought his shotgun with him and bagged a couple of francolin and a duck by a pond we passed, so we had plenty to eat.

I lay in the dark that night looking up at the stars twinkling like a million diamonds strewn across a black velvet cloth in a jeweller's shop window, listening to the crickets sawing out their incessant song, hearing the occasional hoot in the distance from a prowling hyena and wondering about the man we were going to meet. The locals called him *Chipembele*. This was the Bemba name for a rhinoceros, and the locals called him that because he only ever met problems head-on like that eponymous pachyderm.

Shiwa Ngandu, his home, was an out-of-the-way sort of place, difficult to get to. At first glance, it looked like an English country house that had been plonked down in the African bush with lines of Italianate cypress trees beside the drive, a garden full of flowering plants and shrubs, trimmed hedges, and neat lawns. The house itself was made of baked bricks, the courses carefully pointed. It had latticed windows with stone mullions, two storeys, a balcony, a tiled roof, and even a tower. A jumble of African style huts behind the main house gave the place an African flavour, but it was otherwise very old world English, like something you might find down a leafy Home Counties lane.

Colonel Gore-Brown was a great bull of a man. I was never quite sure if he was totally bald or if he shaved his head, but on his short neck, it looked like a polished brown nut, his round face creased by an ever-present smile. He was welcoming and genial, most interested in Dad's mission and willing to help. Among his Bemba tribesmen he was certain he could find good recruits. A couple of trips out to villages confirmed this, and Dad arranged to send a formal recruiting team under one of his company commanders. In the meantime, our host agreed to compile a list of likely candidates.

We stayed for four days before heading home via the Kafue Game Park. Gore-Browne knew Gerry Taylor well for they were two of a kind. He was pleased to show us around his farm and encouraged his workers to explain their work. They all seemed happy and competent and his farm worked as smoothly as the army depot in Lusaka. Mum marvelled at the fields of pretty flowers he was growing and was amazed to discover that they were Pyrethrum, grown to make agricultural insecticide.

WHEN SCHOOL RESUMED, we had a different bus driver. This man was a uniformed soldier from the Motor Transport Pool, and he took no nonsense from us. Corporal Moshembi was unflappable and ignored the fact that I climbed onto the bus one morning holding a large frog I had caught by the roadside. He merely glanced at it and turned away to indicate his disinterest. I might not be able to scare him out of his seat with a *kalilombe* as I had with the last driver, but I wondered how he'd react to a snake.

One morning on the way up to school, as the bus approached the *kopje* where the road went through the cleft, at the same spot where we had had the flat tyre at the end of last term, we had to stop because the road was blocked by a parked Land Rover pick-up. There was nobody in it or nearby. It was a battered old vehicle, painted red and covered in dents and dirt. From the junk in the back, it looked likely to belong to one of the local farmers.

Corporal Moshembi went to look at the vehicle, to see if there was any way of moving it, but the cab door was locked. He came back to the bus and hooted his horn a few times, hoping the Land Rover's driver would return.

Nothing happened.

After about five minutes, we heard a loud bang. The sound echoed round the cleft, bouncing off the hard rockface. Somebody at the back of the bus said it was probably a hunter trying to shoot the man-eating leopard that lived in the rocks. We'd all heard the story, but none of us really believed it. So we were all surprised a few minutes later when a large white man with a rifle in his hand came around the side of the rock and approached the old Land Rover. Draped over his shoulders he carried a large, very dead leopard.

The driver tried to stop us, but he stood no chance, as we surged off the bus to have a look, crowding round the farmer, wanting to touch the cat. It turned out to be an old beast, with broken teeth, mangy fur, and several claws missing. It had obviously had a hard life and, finding the local farm stock easier prey than catching wild animals, had taken to pillaging the corrals, stealing goats and chickens. No humans had ever been killed by this leopard, but that may have been more by chance. Clearly, if a human had been the easiest prey, he would have killed. Now its reign of terror had come to an end, with a bullet from the farmer's rifle exploding in its brain.

The leopard provided a hot topic of conversation on the bus for several weeks before we moved on to other interests. It was to resurface many years later, in the most unexpected of places.

15 ~ Map-reading and jungle training

IN THE EARLY 1950s, trouble erupted in Malaya, where communist insurgents were trying to overthrow the government. Most of them were said to be Chinese bandits, sneaking down the country from the north through the jungle. Britain, as the colonial power, had deployed soldiers to counter the insurgency. As well as sending troops from home, they also sent soldiers from the colonies. Several regiments of Indian soldiers had served with distinction in the jungles of Burma during the Second World War. Now it was the turn of the African regiments to provide troops.

The King's African Rifles, from Kenya and Uganda, were already serving in the Malayan jungle. Then it would be the turn of the Rhodesian Regiments, so jungle training began. The best place for this in Northern Rhodesia was in the Itigu-Sumbu forest in the far north of the country. Here thickly wooded hills and valleys covered the countryside. There were numerous large trees in the river valleys, and thickets so dense it made movement difficult. It was the nearest thing to the Malayan jungle, and ideal training country for the army exercises.

The *askaris* left for their jungle training the week before term ended, singing, smiling men, seated in the backs of three-ton lorries in a long convoy. We watched them go past before our school bus followed them up the northbound road. The nuns were not pleased that most of their pupils were late for school that morning, and spent the first half hour lecturing us about punctuality. When I protested that we were late because of the troop movement, I got my head slapped and was made to stand in the corner for the next half hour. Since I had a pencil in my hand when I was slapped, I kept it, and after a few moments started drawing funny faces and writing on the whitewashed wall. I was careful not to press too hard, so someone had to be quite close to see my pictures. At break time, I started taking bets on how long it would take for the nuns to notice.

It was the last day of term before my scribbles were detected, by which time a number of other people had done time in the corner, so the nuns couldn't say for certain who had put the drawings there. But they knew, and I knew they knew. They just couldn't prove it.

I relished my victory, however small.

The day after school ended, Dad said he was going north to see how the jungle training was getting along. He asked if I would like to go too. Of course I leapt at the chance, and we set off in an army vehicle with a driver. Mum was involved in a committee by that time, running mother and infant clinics for the wives of soldiers. She also played tennis with other European wives in the afternoons, so she stayed in Lusaka. Alistair, of course, was back at his school in Scotland and wouldn't arrive until the following week.

The nearer we got to the Itigu-Sumbu forest, the more the countryside changed. What had been broad open plains became rolling country, crossed by lots of small streams and one or two larger ones. Further north, the gradients became steeper and the valleys deeper. Over the millennia and after intense seasonal rainfall, the streams had carved valleys two hundred feet deep and up to half a mile wide. Large trees filled the valley bottoms and an undergrowth of bushes and smaller trees made quite dense jungle. The upper slopes were covered in dense thorny thickets, with occasional clear patches from which you could look out over the surrounding countryside or, more accurately, over the surrounding treetops.

An exercise was in progress when we arrived and we sat on a hilltop watching. There was almost nothing to see, but trees and yet more trees, some wearing crowns of brilliant yellow or red flowers, others textured with different shades of green. Although there was no discernible activity to my untutored eyes, somehow Dad and the other observers seemed to know what was going on and where things were happening. Movements on the ground were betrayed by flocks of birds taking flight, or troops of monkeys racing across the canopy, making the green sea ripple as the topmost branches moved under their weight. Occasional coloured flares shot skyward from the green sea, trailing thin white tails of smoke.

After a while, Dad left me in the care of Major Jean Salazar and went down into the valley to observe the action from close quarters. He took a radio with him and we listened to his progress and comments as he moved down the slope. After a while we heard he had caught up with a platoon preparing to fell a large tree with explosives, to make a bridge across a fast-flowing stream. Dad gave coordinates, and told us to watch out for it in about five minutes.

"But how will you know where to look?" I asked.

"Your Dad gave us the position of the tree they're blowing

Looking over the Itigu-Sumbu forest.

up," Major Salazar explained, pointing to a spot on his map. He then showed me what the coordinates meant, and how to translate them to the map. His words opened a book of magic for me. That a string of numbers could so precisely locate something on a map was nothing short of miraculous. The nuns in school had spent a lot of time lecturing us about miracles the previous week, and they all sounded pretty unlikely to me. I found it hard to believe in any of them. But if the chosen tree blew up and crashed down across the river at the appointed time, I thought, that would be a decent miracle. I'd believe that.

The observers on the hill had a line of telescopes mounted on tripods. Major Salazar told me to look through his. The tree that was supposed to fall was right in the centre of the viewfinder.

Over the radio, we could hear a countdown and as the numbers decreased to zero I held my breath. Zero came, and nothing happened. Half a second later, flocks of birds rose from canopies surrounding the target tree. Moments later, the tree seemed to grow ten feet taller. Then it sank back and began to topple sideways. A few seconds later the deep boom of an explosion reached us, followed by the angry shrieks of birds and screaming monkeys as they raced away through the treetops and the tearing sound of tangled foliage crashing down. A distinct gash opened up in the lumpy green surface of the forest canopy.

That was proof enough for me that miracles do happen. I had just witnessed one. Now I could tell the nuns.

Seeing he had caught my interest, Major Salazar went on to explain how maps told the shape of the ground, the steepness of the slopes, and where the rivers and streams flowed, all by little coloured lines. He showed me the key with symbols for prominent landmarks, all of which could help identify places. He demonstrated how to find your own position by drawing a compass bearing from a landmark and following it backwards to where it intersected one from another landmark. And he taught me how to use a prismatic compass to take those bearings. When I understood that with a map and a compass I could find my way from anywhere to somewhere else and know what the country would be like along the way, it felt as if I had been given a box of treasure.

Yes, Major Salazar knew what real miracles were.

Dad came back to the ridge as the sun was setting. He sat patiently while I told him all I had learned. When I finished, he grinned and said that now I had learned how the system worked, I needed to learn how to do it while moving. Tomorrow he would give me the coordinates, and I could lead him down to Major Salazar's camp. I had been so absorbed in telling Dad everything I'd learned that afternoon, that I had completely failed to notice the major's departure.

In the morning, it soon became obvious that reading maps while on the move was not as simple as it was from a fixed point.

But my interest had been fired and I was determined to learn. I understood the principle well enough and it was now a matter of practice to get good at applying it. Practice took time, and many, many mistakes. I managed to get us lost a number of times that day, but slowly gained competence.

I have never regretted the lesson.

We spent three days in the jungle and I was thrilled by the experience. There were all sorts of new animals to discover, and different plants. The *askaris* showed me vines which, when cut, contained water that was fit to drink. At first I didn't understand why they couldn't just drink the water from the streams; after all, there were enough of them. But a taste of stream water soon taught me. Many streams tasted foul. It was something to do with the soil they flowed over and the rotting vegetation that made up the forest floor and, as one *askari* pointed out, indicating a large pile of steaming dung on a game trail, animals often left their droppings in the streams.

Little did I realise then that providing clean drinking water in the soggy environment of a rain forest would be an important part of my work one day in the future.

16 ~ Malaya

THE TIME CAME FOR THE regiment to go to Malaya. Dad was leading the advance party, comprising a few officers and about thirty *askaris*. Their job was to liaise with the Kenyan troops they were relieving and prepare base facilities, ready for the regiment's arrival. Most of the troops were going by sea, a journey that would take about three weeks. It involved going by rail to the coast, catching a troop ship to Singapore, and then another train to their operating base up-country. Since this was a full regimental deployment, officers' families were going too. Mum and I were to travel on the troop ship.

One bright morning, we went to Lusaka airport to see Dad and the advance party off. The airport was a fairly informal place in those days: we drove our car right up to where the aeroplane, a four-engined Handley Page Hastings with RAF markings, sat in front of the control tower.

Mum, who was normally so bright and happy, looked very worried and crest-fallen after we said our goodbyes. I couldn't think what had upset her, but then I didn't understand what it must feel like having to say goodbye to your soulmate as he headed off to war, again. She'd been through all this before, only eleven years previously, when he had left her in Fattigerh, in northern India, and taken his Indian soldiers off to fight the Japanese in Burma. They thought all that had ended long ago. It was not until I joined the RAF in 1966 that she ever let on how frightened she'd been that day as we watched the aircraft manoeuvre on the ground like a huge silver moth, blowing dust and grit all over us when it turned to speed down the runway and lift into the empty blue sky.

I was excited. Mum, poor thing, felt bereft and empty inside as she clung onto me.

She kept me close for the next few days because the house felt empty. Not only was Dad not there, Samson had gone with him, and we missed his cheery, smiling presence almost as much. But the gloom didn't last long as other wives came around and Mum started thinking about packing up the house. She sent for our crates from the army stores, and began collecting things together to go in each box. She had a system for packing, with lots of lists

The advance party prepares to board the RAF Handley Page Hastings which would take them to Malaya. This aircraft (503) now sits in the Allied Air Museum in Berlin.

The troop train to Dar es Salam crossed two game reserves.

and her own particular order for doing things. She put me to work carrying and wrapping under her instructions. It certainly kept me busy and, although we only spent the mornings packing, within a week we'd piled our whole household into boxes, ready to go into storage. All that remained was what was going to Malaya with us, and that could all fit in three trunks and a couple of suitcases.

Fortunately I had never been a child endowed with a huge pile of toys. It wasn't that my parents had been mean and deprived me of anything, but money had never been plentiful and anyway, I found my playthings outside in the garden and in the bush. I wasn't much interested in most of the toys other children had. So I wasn't in any way inconvenienced by all this packing up. When it was time to leave, my only sadness was in leaving friends like Robert, Gilbert and Nasouma behind. The families of the African troops were not coming with us.

A long convoy of army lorries took us to the railway station where a chartered troop train was waiting. A freight train had left the day before, taking huge piles of equipment and a few troops. Our train took the bulk of the troops and the few European fam-

The troopship MV Devonshire *in which we travelled to Malaya.*

ilies who had elected to go. Some of the European families, it seemed, were staying in Lusaka.

This train moved much faster than the one which had brought us from Cape Town to Lusaka. Perhaps being a military train had something to do with it, and the distance was shorter to Dar es Salam, where we were to board the ship. It only took two days.

The bush on this trip was far more interesting than the empty spaces of the open veldt in South Africa. Here it was mainly parkland, with lots of small trees and only occasional patches of open savannah. Our route north went through Kasama and then crossed into Tanganyika and onward through Kibeya and Kitadu to the sea at Dar. Nobody ever gave our destination its full name.

The port was a smelly place, but exciting as well, with ships in the harbour tied up at the wharves, cranes swinging great baled loads in and out of their holds, tug boats moving about and hooting, other ships anchored offshore and a general air of bustle and activity. The railway line brought us right onto the quay, alongside the troopship. The gangplanks were already crowded, with porters carrying luggage on board and others coming off.

Our vessel, the troopship MV *Devonshire*, looked huge, its one large funnel sticking up high above the towering body of the ship. It was painted white, with a broad royal blue line along the side, just below the top one of four rows of portholes. The paint-work that from a distance looked pristine and gleaming white was, on closer inspection, tired and showing signs of rust where old paint was flaking, but this mattered little. It was still an impos-ing sight. Lifeboats dangled from davits above the upper deck and a covered walkway ran down the outside of the main deck, from the open foredeck right to the back of the ship. Two tall masts supported a network of jibs, wires and aerials and a column of smoky fumes rose from the fat funnel that topped everything.

There were staterooms on the upper deck, together with bars and a lounge for the first-class passengers. Being only dependant families, we and the two other officers' families travelling with us didn't qualify for such luxury. We had cabins just below the main deck, with portholes just above the blue line. The *askaris* were crowded into the decks below, in large dormitories like barrack blocks, mess halls and recreational rooms. Their conditions, while not luxurious, were nevertheless better than they had at home. The only difference was they were bachelor quarters.

Our mess hall was on the main deck, behind a day lounge and bar staffed by uniformed sailors. While we had the run of most of the ship, we were discouraged from going onto the foredeck which was reserved for the *askaris* to do physical exercises and get some fresh air four times a day in their companies. Since none of them had ever been to sea before, many were seasick for the first few days, but plentiful food, fresh air, and exercise soon had them

Bullock cart in Ceylon pulled by two young water buffalo.

back in shape. Often they would sing as they did their exercises and the familiar sound of their voices lifted everyone's spirits.

From Dar, the ship went Sri Lanka – Ceylon as it was then called – where we waited for three days in Colombo. The *askaris* had to remain within the confines of the docks, so they went ashore each day and marched up and down the quay for exercise. We were allowed to go out into the town on excursions. My memories of our time there are few, but one sight that stuck in my mind was the bullock carts, many with arched rattan covers, all with huge wooden wheels and pulled by heavy grey water buffalo or hump-backed oxen. Compared to the wild African buffalo, which is a very dangerous and aggressive animal, the water buffalo looked lethargic, passive, and positively world-weary. They spent most of their time dreamily chewing the cud, their heads hung low under the weight of heavy horns and the wooden yokes pressing down on their necks.

In Colombo, we saw elephants in the streets. They were disappointing after the huge beasts I had seen in the Kafue Game

Park; small, dingy animals with humped backs, small ears, and diminutive tusks. They lacked the dignity and poise of their African cousins. Almost all the elephants here were being ridden, generally by a small brown man in a loincloth wielding a sharp pointed metal rod. To my mind, they looked out of place walking around the crowded streets, but few people seemed to pay them much attention and Mum assured me that tame elephants like this were common throughout India, where they were used for heavy pulling work.

The *Devonshire* was an old ship. She didn't travel fast and had taken seven days to get to Colombo from Dar. It was to take a further nine days to get to Singapore and a few people, many of them young National Service officers, were getting bored in the confined environment. To relieve the boredom, somebody organised a tour of the ship, so that they might learn something of how a vessel of this nature functioned. Led by one of the ship's crew, who explained about each place where they paused on the way round, the tour gradually descended through the decks to the engine room, deep in the bowels of the ship. By the time they got down there, Major Salazar, who had only gone along to set an example to the younger officers, was bored stiff and in dire need of excitement. Looking up through the clattering machinery at the maze of pipes, cables, ladders, and gantries overhead, he saw through the aperture of the funnel a small patch of blue sky, far above. A ladder bolted to the inside of the funnel caught his eye and sparked a new thought.

"Pay attention!" he yelled. "Everyone up top as fast as you can. Last one to the top deck bar buys the drinks," he shouted. "Go!"

Saying this, he scrambled up the nearest stanchion, swinging himself upwards like a monkey as the others on the tour scrambled over one another to reach the ladder by which they had descended. Up he went, using the machinery, ladders, whatever offered a handhold and a route upwards, until he reached the ladder going up the funnel. Ignoring the heat and rising clouds of fumes, he climbed, right up the inside of the funnel. This being the main exhaust stack for all the engines, plus the escape route for any excess steam, it became increasingly hot and airless the further he climbed. But he was determined not to be the last man in the bar. In fact he was determined to be the first one there by several drinks.

Reaching the top and fresh air, he rolled himself over the edge, only to find that there was no ladder on the outside to facilitate his descent. Undeterred, he got both legs over the rim and let go. It was only about twenty-five feet to the deck. He landed with a thump, twisted an ankle, and tumbled sideways into a ventilator, which cracked two ribs and broke his arm. The bar was on the deck below, so he crawled to the nearest companion way and slid down the steps to the deck below. The bottom of the companion way ladder was right next to the door into the bar. Crawling inside, he hauled himself up by the bar and ordered a drink. By the time the first officer arrived from the engine room, he had already downed a stiff brandy and was sitting on a stool sipping a nice cold beer. It was only when the others looked at him closely they realised the heat inside the funnel had singed off almost all his hair, his eyebrows and most of his moustache, and steamed him to a deep lobster pink. But he didn't have to buy the drinks!

This was but one of innumerable mad japes Jean Salazar indulged in, but, it must be said, he never asked any of his soldiers, be they officer or *askari*, to do anything dangerous he wasn't fully prepared and willing to do himself. He always led by example and his men would follow him anywhere. Although he was reluctant to talk about it, it had been his willingness to take risks himself that won him a Military Cross during the war in Burma. I only learned the facts of this many years later.

On a night patrol to scout a Japanese position, Salazar realised it was surrounded by machine gun pits. Instructing his men to start a brew, he crept forward alone to check the lie of the land. Almost immediately, he found one of these pits. Crawling round behind, he dropped a grenade into the pit and moved on, discovering a large fuel dump a quarter of a mile beyond. He placed several grenades in strategic positions and withdrew, pulling behind him strings attached to the grenade safety pins. At a safe distance he gave a sharp pull, removing the safety pins and then rose and ran directly for the machine gun pit where he had dropped the first grenade. Jumping in to avoid the explosion that was about to go off behind him, he discovered it was the wrong pit and he landed on three Japanese soldiers who were very much alive. Fortunately he had a bayonet in his hand and the boom of the exploding fuel depot which accompanied his abrupt arrival gave him the advantage of surprise. Five minutes later, behaving as if nothing unusual had happened, he crawled back into the cover where his men had just made the tea. At dawn they found the fuel depot had been destroyed and the Japanese company had withdrawn from the area.

17 ~ Raffles Hotel and Penang

IT WAS DARK WHEN the *Devonshire* docked in Singapore and we saw very little of the port as a rickety army bus was waiting to take us and our baggage to a hotel.

The hotel looked very imposing from the outside and the entrance hall was very grand. This was the fabled Raffles Hotel. The adults were allowed to use the public rooms and the famous Long Bar, but we children were confined to an annexe that was less luxurious but still surrounded by elegant palm trees and bright flowering hibiscus bushes. After being cooped up on the ship for the best part of three weeks, it was good to be on dry land again and it didn't take me long to find a source of adventure.

The streets nearby all had huge storm drains beside them, with ducts passing under the roadway to join the two sides together. These drains mostly had a few inches of water in the bottom and smelled pretty foul, but that did not put me off exploring. I soon discovered there was a whole community of children scurrying about these channels, collecting things that had been discarded, gathering small blooms that grew in their margins to sell on the street in little bunches for a few coppers, and chasing the ever-pres-

Raffles Hotel as it is today, We stayed here for our first three weeks in Malaya.

ent rats. It seemed like fun and whenever I was not being supervised I would sneak off to join them. It didn't take long to find my way around, and the catapult which had remained idle in the back pocket of my shorts soon proved its worth against the rats. Our lack of a common language was no deterrent to communal interests, and being able to stun or kill a rat from twenty feet away was a skill that got noticed. The local kids soon copied my weapon, using bits of old bicycle inner tube for the elastic, and sticks broken from nearby bushes for their yokes. Rat hunting became a regular competition whenever Mum and the other wives took to the tennis court, which was most afternoons around four o'clock.

After three weeks we moved on from Singapore. The troops, who had been housed in barracks at Changi, the military base at the east end of the island, boarded a long train. We had a compartment in a rear carriage for the two-day trip up through Malaya to Penang. It was made all the more uncomfortable by the

We were soon bored of the rows of trees in rubber plantations.

heavy steel plates with small slots in them which were pulled up over the windows as protection against bandit attacks whenever we passed through a patch of jungle or a large plantation. The train also had three open trucks with machine guns mounted on them, manned by alert *askaris* whenever the train was moving. Since most of countryside on the journey was either through regimented plantations of rubber trees, which soon became dull and tedious to look at, or through patches of dense jungle where the bandits loved to attack the line and blow up trains, the safety plates were closed a lot of the time, so it was a hot and airless trip.

Fortunately our journey north was uneventful and we arrived late at night to be taken by rickshaw to our accommodation, our baggage following in a second rickshaw pulled by a wiry little man with amazingly strong legs. Our house was just along the road from Tokong Ular, the Snake Temple. Accustomed to the simplicity of African huts, I found this an incredibly ornate building, with upturned eaves and raised corners on its tiled roofs, strange dragon statues all over the place, and so many colours it looked like a rainbow. The temple was built on a platform surrounded by a low wall, with gardens to the sides and back, and wide steps at the front for devotees and visitors to climb.

Inside there were ledges and shelves on every wall, with numerous wooden structures, much like hat stands, that had snakes of an infinite variety draped over them. The air was thick with incense and vibrated with the almost constant hum of low, chanting voices. Although I soon recognised the large pythons draped over some heavy railings, most of the snakes were unfamiliar to me. Some were very brightly coloured. The railings for the pythons and boas were strong and heavy as these were huge snakes, some over fifteen feet long. They were far bigger than any I'd seen in the African bush.

Seeing one very pretty golden coloured snake, I was stretching out my hand to touch it when I received a sharp whack across my arm from a stick. Turning to see who had assaulted me, I found a wizened old monk with a shaven head, grinning like a gargoyle and shaking his head.

"Berry bad, berry bad," he said. "No touchy." He made biting gestures, screwed up his face in an agonised grimace, and then mimed slumping to the floor.

I got the message. This one was venomous.

I pointed to another pretty snake and made stroking gestures and this time the monk smiled, lifted the serpent from the frame where it was coiled and laid it across my hands. He watched carefully as I examined the snake and then pointed to several others that were safe to handle. I got to know that old monk well over the next few months, as I was a frequent visitor to the temple, but somehow I never discovered his name.

Tokong Ular was home to hundreds of serpents of many different varieties, a lot of them poisonous. While visitors were permitted to handle the snakes, surprisingly few people ever got bitten and I wondered if this might be because the snakes were drugged. The strong scent of incense had a calming effect on everyone who entered and I imagined the snakes lived in a happy narcotic haze.

Whenever the temple received a new snake, the old monk made a point of showing it to me, having discerned that I was both interested and unafraid. He taught me how to handle them gently, but seemed a little dismayed when I indicated how I would normally remove the fangs from any venomous snake I caught. He made it plain that these were sacred snakes, and that was not permissible here. Their fangs and venomous capacity would remain intact. This was a salutary lesson, which made me view both snakes in general and the monks who lived among them in a whole new light.

After a week or two I was sent to a local school to continue where the nuns in Lusaka had left off. School here was more fun, although I missed my friends, who had been my best school mates. Classes only occupied the mornings so, with little to do in the afternoons, it was not long before I discovered the old Chinese game of Mah Jongg and learned to play.

Mum had bought a set in Singapore and, having learned to play years before when she lived in India, soon found others to form a regular group when they couldn't play tennis. I played with school friends until I discovered a regular Mah Jongg game running in one of the Chinese shops round the corner from the school. What made this more exciting was that they played for real money. I saved up my few cents of pocket money and went gambling.

I'm not sure if it was the Chinese women being kind to a

beginner, or whether I was good at the game, but my few cents soon grew into dollars and before long I had a fistful of notes. Dad was home from the jungle for a few weeks, and I knew he would take a dim view of my gambling, so I hid the cash in an old cracked teapot which I stuffed into a hole in the outer wall of the snake temple, retrieving it each time I went to play with the Chinese market women and hiding it again before going home.

I managed to keep this up for about four months before I was discovered, and then it was purely by chance. Mum decided one afternoon that instead of going to the tennis club she would explore some of the Chinese shops in the bazaar with two of her friends. They came into the shop where I was playing in the back room just as I called Mah Jongg on a really good hand that was worth a lot of money. My shrieks of delight and the general cheering of the Chinese women attracted her attention. She stood in the doorway, hands on her hips and looking cross, demanding to know what I was doing and telling me sharply to come home at once.

"No, no, missy, no take him now!" my playing partners all chorused. "He winning big time. Can't stop now!"

I could see Mum was trying very hard not to laugh, and didn't know what to do as I pleaded to be allowed to play just a little longer.

"Okay, one more wall," she conceded, sitting on a chair offered by the shopkeeper to watch.

Busy hands swirled the tiles, nimble fingers rebuilt the wall and we were off again, lost in the game. I managed to call Mah Jongg again, but this time found my hand was worth so little I had to pay out a small amount rather than raking in the lolly. As we walked home, Mum asked me how I could keep track when the women played so fast.

"It's easy, you just look at the tiles," I said.

"But they don't have any numbers on them," she remarked.

It was the first time I had realised we had been playing with a Chinese set that had no Roman numerals on the tiles. No wonder she was confused.

Dad, home again from another patrol in the jungle, didn't approve of my gambling and made me donate the contents of my teapot to the Snake Temple. The old monk who had so often been my guide there received the gift with great solemnity and obvious delight. He insisted on making Dad and me sit while he served us green tea, handing each of us a snake to hold while he prepared it. Dad looked most uncomfortable with this and as soon as courtesy would permit, made excuses and left, telling me not to be late home.

We also spent time at the lido in Penang. There I swam for the first time in salt water. I didn't like the taste and it stung my eyes, but I soon learned to keep my mouth and eyes shut. The one disadvantage this had was that we also encountered occasional poisonous sea snakes and puffer fish. A stab from one of the spines of a puffer fish if it inflated itself against you could be excruciatingly painful and incapacitate you for weeks. These little peskies where normally quite small, being broad of head and only a few inches long. Most of them were a sandy colour along the back, with little black spots and a white belly. While never pretty, they looked innocent enough until upset or threatened. Then they inflated themselves in a matter of seconds to become large spiny globes, six or eight inches in diameter.

It was also fun to swim in the sea. Unfortunately that was where these spiny denizens also swam, and they were unreasonably common, as were the sea snakes. Avoiding them called for agility. My swimming improved rapidly.

18 ~ Africa again

WE WERE IN PENANG FOR only nine months before the regiment returned to Rhodesia. Most of the *askaris* had spent almost half that time in the jungle, with companies alternating on monthly patrols. They went in carrying a fortnight's rations and ammunition and supplemented their food with the bounty of the forest. They received additional supplies by parachute drop from time to time, but basically they had to be self-sufficient. The Rhodesian soldiers adapted well to this environment and had a good record of success fighting the Chinese bandits, capturing some of their important leaders and killing others. Even so, they were pleased when it came time to leave and they were a merry band when they embarked on the troopship once again, knowing they were homeward bound. We travelled on HMT *Nevasa* this time. She was the flagship of the trooping fleet, nearly new and much more comfortable than the *Devonshire* had been.

On the trip back to Mombasa, we hit four heavy storms, which made life miserable for those on the lower decks. The soldiers' relief to be back on African soil was evident. Smiling faces hung from every window on the long train as it left the port, and we enjoyed almost constant singing and drumming all the way back to Lusaka.

It was good to get back, and better still to see my friends again. Mum unpacked our boxes again and set up house in the same one we had left less than a year earlier. The garden, which she had so lovingly tended before, had been neglected and was overgrown, but the crested cranes were still in their pen and Nkoti was still there to look after them. His evident delight when I first went down to the cranes' pen, and the welcome I got from Robert, Gilbert and their families made me feel I really had come home. The only person missing was Nasouma.

Soon after we had left for Malaya, news had been received that her grandmother was dying, and her mother had taken her back to the village they came from to care for her. They had not yet returned to Lusaka. It was more than a year before the old lady finally expired, by which time we were moving on again. Nasouma didn't come back to the capital until after we had left to return to Britain. Her absence left a hole in my life as, like Robert and Gilbert, she had been a very special friend.

It was almost twenty years before we were to meet again, and that was on the other side of the continent in Togo.

MY NATURAL INCLINATION was to spend time with the children I knew best, the ones I went to school with, but comments had apparently been made about this. We would soon have to return to Britain as Dad's posting was nearing its end. My parents persuaded me to spend more time among the European children so that I was used to British ways of doing things and wouldn't later feel too much of a misfit.

Children at that age are like sponges, absorbing everything

that's offered, so my English had become passable. This made participation much less of a strain than it had been before. There was also one English girl I rather liked, whose company I sought out whenever I could. Vanessa Bunn was the daughter of one of the company commanders, and I liked her parents too. Since my original girlfriend, Nasouma, had deserted me to return to her village, I adopted Vanessa and at a party one day asked her to marry me. To my delight she said yes. I was not quite seven years old, but knew one had to look to the future, and the future now looked rosy.

Not long after this, our friends the du Viviers announced that they were selling Sheko Farm and returning to Belgium. One of Charles's relations had died and it seemed the family brewing business needed him at home. The farm was also not doing so well because the world prices of both maize and tobacco had fallen. He had found a buyer and they were almost ready to go. In order to let the new owner move in while the last formalities were completed and a flight back to Europe was arranged, Charles and his family came to stay with us.

On the day of their departure, we all went to the airport to see them off. Charles drove his family to the airport in the big blue Chevrolet he had bought when he sold Dad the old Ford we still used. Dad was going to drive the Chevrolet back to our house and sell it for him. After saying goodbye and watching their plane depart, Dad and I climbed into the Chevrolet while Mum followed in our car. Halfway along the straight road out of the airport, we hit a pothole and the steering broke. The car slewed to the side, careered across the road and, as Dad stamped his foot on the pedal, the brakes also failed. We ended up with a jolt, nose down in a deep storm drain, jammed up against the windscreen by the front bench seat, which had come away from its mountings.

At the time, we didn't realise it had been removed on the farm a few days before, to get something large into the back, and had never been properly bolted back in position.

A crowd of Africans soon surrounded the vehicle and pulled the seat off, releasing us. Apart from an interesting collection of bruises that turned spectacularly blue and yellow over the next few days, neither of us had sustained any injury. We'd only been doing about thirty-five miles an hour, so we were lucky.

Dad chose two of the small boys from the crowd of onlookers and commissioned them to stay and guard the Chevrolet until a rescue truck arrived. He gave each of them two shillings. This was enormous wealth to the two lads, to whom a few coppers would have made them rich, and the promise that they would get the same again if the car was intact when the rescue truck arrived ensured it would be well guarded.

We climbed into our own car and Mum drove us home.

A few weeks later, we made a trip to Kenya to visit Dad's brother Bill who was serving with the King's African Rifles. He and his solders had been in the Malayan jungle when we first got there, and they handed over their duties and patrols to the Northern Rhodesian regiment.

Dad and Bill went into the jungle on a two-week reconnaissance patrol together, taking only their two senior sergeants and a couple of *askaris* from each regiment with them. During this patrol, Bill had been able to brief Dad on vital intelligence that, a few weeks later, enabled the Rhodesian soldiers to capture an important MPLA terrorist commander, together with his bed. Bill had warned Dad about this man and had been most insistent that they should capture his bed with him. When it was examined, the hollow tubes it was made from were found to contain all sorts of important plans, maps and logistical details that enabled many more bandits to be rounded up.

Now both were back in Africa and, although Bill was involved in mopping up operations after the Mau Mau emergency, both would soon be returning to Europe. Dad received a posting to the Ministry of Defence in London and Bill to France to serve in the Supreme Headquarters of the Allied Powers of Europe (SHAPE) at Fontainebleau.

We'd made the trip up to Kenya a few years previously and enjoyed seeing the wide-open spaces of the Masai Mara and the teeming herds of antelope and gazelle. The vastness of it all made the game parks in Northern Rhodesia, which were still in their infancy as wildlife reserves, seem somewhat sparse and immature, despite having the more interesting scenery.

Uncle Bill had married a French lady, Jeannine Goerger, who added a lot of style to the otherwise slightly boring European military community in Kenya. Coming from such very different backgrounds, she and my mother never entirely hit it off. They were always friendly enough, but you couldn't describe them as soul mates. This was hardly surprising since Jeannine was well educated and had an illustrious heritage with a string of generals in her ancestry. Her father had been a district governor in Morocco before becoming André Citroen's right-hand man during his great Croisière Jaune expedition to China. Mum's origins had been much more humble. Her father had been a sergeant in Dad's regiment while it was in India, where she spent most of her formative years.

Fluent in several European languages, Jeannine decided only to speak French to me, thereby opening another new door and equipping me with a language that has been in constant use all my life. Later, when we were all back in Europe, my brother and I spent some of our school holidays with Bill and Jeannine in Paris – but I'm getting ahead of myself.

BACK IN LUSAKA, life settled down again and it was back to school with the nuns for me. After the freedom and colour of the Chinese school in Penang, this was like being sent to prison. But at least I had my African friends around me.

It wasn't to last. A few weeks later, we got the definitive date for Dad's posting back to Britain. Our departure was imminent so the boxes once again came out of the store, and once again Mum packed up our home. This was to be a feature of our family life for many years to come. She really was an ace packer. In less than a week, she had the crates ready for the man who came with a pot of paint and stencils to apply new addresses on them, and a coil of metal ribbon and steel banding clamp to seal them.

While nothing had been said, something told me Britain would be different, and I wanted to maximise what time I had left for doing what I loved. As our departure date approached I spent as much time as I could rambling in the bush with my friends. I spent a lot of time at their houses, ate with their families and often slept there.

It was during one of these occasions that the *nganga* arrived. Everything stopped and everyone present fell silent. He was the uncle, the same man who had stared at me that day after we had been skinny dipping in the stream, the man who had been Charles du Vivier's tractor driver at Sheko Farm. His arrival sent a frisson of excitement through the family, but it also raised the hairs on the back of our necks as the presence of such men can be uncomfortable. They carried an aura of mystery with them because of their special and esoteric powers, and maintained an atmosphere of uncertainty until they had everyone's attention fully under their control.

Seeing me seated with the family, dipping my hand in the food pot with them, he announced that I should be adopted because I behaved more like an African child than a European one. He took hot coals from the cooking fire and put them into an empty earthenware pot. Adding herbs from pouches stuffed into his pockets and inside his shirt, he produced clouds of aromatic smoke which filled the *rondavel*. It made me feel dizzy at first, but after a few moments the effect cleared. Although it was dark inside the hut, I seemed to be able to see more clearly and looked around to see who was holding the lamp. There was no lamp.

The *nganga* began reciting words that made no sense to me and I realised he was talking to the sprits. Fascinated and slightly apprehensive, I sat and listened. He placed the pot of smouldering herbs in my hands and I noticed that the outside of the pot felt cold, despite the glowing embers within. What had started with an element of fear soon changed because the warm drone of his voice felt like a cloak was being draped round my shoulders. It gave me a feeling of belonging I can remember clearly to this day. The fact that I didn't understand his words didn't matter; it sounded right.

From a pot of goo that was also secreted about his person, the *nganga* dabbed white paste on my forehead, cheeks, shoulders and chest as he chanted. When he was finished, all the Chileshe family took turns to hug me and repeat some strange words.

As the family resumed their places, more food was passed round. I looked round for the *nganga*, but he had gone, vanished like a spirit. The smoke from the smouldering herbs had all cleared and the atmosphere in the hut was back to normal.

I turned to Gilbert and asked what all this had all been about.

"You've been adopted," he said. "That was an initiation ceremony. You are now part of our family and our clan."

I felt honoured and confused in equal measure. Honoured because it felt important to be so accepted; confused because nobody had asked or invited me, and I wasn't sure what my parents would have to say about it. Had they been asked? If I'd known in advance what was going to happen, I would have paid more attention to remember the details better. When I mentioned this to Gilbert he laughed, saying I wouldn't have been able to remember more. That was what the smoke from the pot was for, to dull the memory of the person being initiated. I felt slightly cheated by this, but he assured me it was always the same, and part of the ritual. Later, when boys faced circumcision, they would be asked to recall this ceremony and the amount they remembered would influence other factors throughout their lives.

"But I've already been circumcised," I protested.

"There will still come an occasion when you will be called to remember, never fear."

Gilbert suggested I might want to be careful how I mentioned the initiation to my family when I got home. Many European parents might object because they didn't understand, but having got to know mine well, he thought they might be all right with it as they seemed to be much more comfortable with the native traditions.

Since we were getting ready to leave Northern Rhodesia, I decided to wait before saying anything to anyone, although Robert, who hadn't been there that evening, clearly knew all about what had happened by the time we went for our daily look at the crested cranes the following afternoon.

19 ~ Back to Britain

OUR DEPARTURE THIS TIME was by air, at least for the first leg of the journey. We flew from Lusaka to Mombasa and boarded a troopship there. Flying was a new experience, and I wasn't sure whether to approach it with trepidation or excitement. There had been a spectacular air crash a few weeks before, and I'd seen pictures of the smashed-up plane in the newspapers. Miraculously only a few people had been killed, along with a flock of goats that happened to be grazing where the plane came down. Even so, the lack of human casualties did nothing to persuade me that flying was without risks.

I needn't have worried. The aircraft was an RAF Hastings, like the one that had taken Dad and his soldiers to Malaya. Sleek and silver on the outside, it was rough and ready inside: a row of small windows down either side; a dozen steel-framed canvas seats facing backwards. Most of the space was given over to cargo. On our flight, there were two propellers strapped to the floor between the seats along with a selection of crates, all tied down by a cargo net.

The noise from the four engines was so loud you had to shout close to someone's ear just to be heard. When the pilot opened the throttles, the noise increased tenfold, isolating each of us in a roaring cocoon. The crew, moving about inside, all wore blue cloth helmets with thick ear pads. We passengers had to stuff bits of cotton wool in our ears, not that it made much difference. Like the propellers and the crates under the net, we too were just cargo.

The take-off was a tremendous thrill. The engines roared and we felt the aircraft begin to roll. Facing backwards as we were, we leaned against our seat straps while through the windows we could see the ground racing past to disappear behind us. As the aircraft lifted, cars, buildings and people got smaller and smaller, looking like toys until they disappeared beneath a layer of white cloud. A few minutes later, sunlight flooded the cabin as we emerged from the top of the clouds. Above us the heavens were a pure, clear blue. Below spread a fluffy white carpet. In our roaring, rocking metal tube, we floated serenely above the world and all sensation of speed disappeared. The only discernible changes were the white carpet slowly dropping away below us and the air inside the cabin becoming much cooler and more bearable.

I was staring out the window, my nose glued to the glass, when I felt someone tugging at my shirt. It was a crew member offering me a blue cloth helmet like his own. When I put it on, he plugged the lead trailing from the helmet into a socket and I could immediately hear his voice. He said the pilot had asked if I would like to go forward and visit the cockpit. I nodded enthusiastically and followed as he clambered over the propellers and the heap of cargo that lay between us and the front of the plane.

Entering the cockpit was like emerging into a world of magic. The view out the windows was much the same as I'd had from the window just behind my seat. It was just that there was so much more of it. The black control panel in front of the pilot was fascinating, with dozens of dials, knobs and switches: little needles quivering as they pointed to tiny white numbers on dials, horizontal bars gently rocking to match the far horizon where the white of the clouds met the blue of the sky. It looked confusing, but then I realised the dials were groups that looked similar, and I began to detect a sense of order in the layout. The noise was less in the cockpit and, with headphones on, I could hear the pilot's explanation of what everything was and how it worked.

At first I stood between the two pilots' seats, but after a few minutes the man in the right-hand seat climbed out and asked if I would like to sit in his place. I was too small to see over the windscreen and a few moments later he came back with a thick cushion, which gave me a much better view. I stayed in the cockpit all the way to Mombasa, relinquishing the seat and standing between the pilots as we descended, then sitting on the floor, holding the back of the pilots' seats as we touched down.

If that experience wasn't guaranteed to give a small boy dreams of flying, I don't know what did, but memory of that flight has endured for a lifetime. I was sad to leave the plane at the airport but, while I hoped there would soon be other opportunities to fly, there was another adventure to look forward to: another sea voyage.

Our ship was the *Nevasa* again, but this time we had a larger cabin because there were three of us. For the first few days, we sailed close to the east coast of Africa through calm tropical seas, the shore just a dim grey line on the horizon to our left, the sea a wide expanse of gently rolling water to our right. After four days, we reached Aden and anchored in the outer harbour.

ADEN WAS A GREY, barren place, the collapsed caldera of an extinct volcano with a tall mountain and a secondary crater as the backdrop to the harbour. On an island in the outer harbour, men were busily building dhows, the traditional Arabian sailing boats. Their wooden hulls showed the various stages of building from naked ribs to sleek, oiled completion as the shipwrights bent thick, hand-sawn planks and secured them in position with heavy copper nails and roves. The scene was a hive of industry, yet it had about it a timeless quality that had been the same for centuries. Even so, in the few hours our ship spent in the harbour, we saw three dhows launched.

Our ship had called at Aden because it was a bunkering port on the route home and there were also passengers joining us there. Still a British colony, Aden had a considerable naval and RAF presence. The harbour was as busy with naval vessels as with the civilian traffic dominated by the constant coming and going of dhows plying routes down the African coast to Durban or across the Arabian Sea to Pakistan, India, and beyond.

Dhow building on Slave Island in Aden harbour.

A tanker barge came alongside almost as soon as our anchor was dropped, and several more followed over the next few hours as the Nevasa filled her tanks with oil. A few passengers went ashore in a small launch. New people came aboard, their luggage being run up the stairway hanging down the ship's side by wiry bronze-bodied porters wearing only a loincloth and a turban.

As the sun headed down to the western horizon, our anchor was pulled up with clanking chains and grumbling machinery. The decks shivered as the screws began to turn and we sailed out of the harbour into the sunset. Behind us, the naked rock of the crater wall glowed pink in the last rays of sunlight.

It was dark as we entered the Red Sea, but in the morning we were treated to a spectacular escort of dolphins riding the ship's bow wave, with others following and playing in our turbulent wake. Three days later, we stopped at Port Suez where we dropped anchor opposite the ornate customs house to wait for other ships to arrive and a convoy to assemble. The Suez Canal was only wide enough to accommodate ships travelling in one direction so going by convoy was the answer. The only passing place was the Great Bitter Lake at the southern end of the waterway.

We had to wait two days for our convoy to assemble and for a line of southbound ships to pass through. During that time, we went ashore to explore the bazaar – and were entertained by the bazaar coming to us. The ship was constantly surrounded by a clutter of small trading boats, their occupants trying to sell all manner of exotic goods to passengers hanging over the ship's rail.

Our passage through the canal was unremarkable, except that we could see the shore close at hand on both sides of the ship. The Egyptian desert consisted of mile upon mile of yellow sand, and I was soon bored by it. Even the occasional camel standing staring at us as we passed did nothing to break the monotony. After the vibrant, smelly, bustling atmosphere of Port Suez, it was a bit of a let-down.

Port Said, at the northern end of the canal, was a welcome relief with bright lights twinkling on the waterfront, loud, raucous Arabic music floating across the water on the still evening air, and small boats bustling about between the large ships. We didn't stop this time, but passed through, out into the open Mediterranean.

Two days later the crew battened down the hatches, screwed the portholes shut, and we sweltered in our cabins or the saloon as the Nevasa ploughed through a heavy storm. Huge waves rolled along the ship's length, submerging most of the portholes, spume lashed across the open decks, the bow alternately rising on a wave and plunging into the following trough in a thumping roller-coaster motion. This went on for nearly two days before the storm cleared and the sea settled to a gently rolling calm and we sailed serenely into Malta's Grand Harbour at Valetta. This was only a brief stop to pick up mail and two passengers. Nobody was allowed off the ship and within hours we were at sea again for the final ten-day passage to Britain.

This being the final leg, the ship took on a party air with a concert and a fancy dress party the evening before we passed Gibraltar. People spent days making costumes and Mum had pieces of material and robes laid out on her bunk in our cabin as she tailored and adjusted, snipped and sewed, making herself an exotic Oriental costume out of silks she had bought the year before in Singapore. She also made a white Pathan's outfit for my Dad, but he had to make his own moustache.

After passing Gibraltar, we endured another storm coming up

Fancy dress parade: Mum, holding the fan, made her costume by hand in four days. She made Dad's too – but not his moustache.

through the Bay of Biscay and finally came onto Plymouth sound on a *driech* grey day. We disembarked straight onto a train which took us to London and a drab hotel where we stayed for three days. In the mornings, Dad disappeared to the War Office to sort out about his new job and to arrange housing for us. Mum and I remained holed up in the hotel with little to do, staring out of the windows at grimy grey streets filled with smelly traffic and crowds of bedraggled people shuffling along rain-swept pavements under black umbrellas. To break the tedium, she took me to Madame Tussaud's and the British Museum and we rode around on the top deck of the big red buses, looking at the city. I didn't see much to interest me, except the flocks of pigeons in Trafalgar Square.

Sunny Africa was never far from our thoughts. Oh, how we missed the fresh *naartjies* we used to buy at fifteen for a shilling, or the paw-paws and mangoes taken fresh from the trees in our own back garden. Here the food was tasteless, with vegetables boiled until they were grey. Meat was stringy and tasteless, and insipid tinned fruit cocktail was the only fruit available.

We missed the vigour and inclusiveness of African life. The streets were crowded but we saw no smiling faces, received no cheery greetings from people we passed. They walked by, looking away, hunching their shoulders and shuffling their feet in the cold, wet streets.

This was November in 1957 and Britain was not an appealing place.

20 ~ An English school

THREE DAYS AFTER ARRIVING in England, we moved to Buckinghamshire. Unseen, Dad had rented a house at Lye Green, a hamlet on top of the hill a few miles from Chesham. It was a sprawling house with a good-sized garden including an acre and a half of woods at the back. Our nearest neighbour, Lye Green House, was the only other house at one end of the open space after which the hamlet was named. This was a large building, mostly hidden behind a tall laurel hedge, inhabited by an old couple we never actually met. They emerged once a week, seated in state in the back of a shiny, black, chauffeur-driven Austin Princess.

A rough lane ran down the side of the wood behind our house. It led to a small farm owned by Geoff and Betty Copping. Geoff was a small bright man, who worked for the Post Office at Dollis Hill. He was an electrical engineer, specialising in the relatively new field of electronics, and was involved in the design and development of the second generation ERNIE, the Electronic Random Number Indicating Equipment which picked the winning numbers for the monthly Premium Bonds draw. In his spare time, he was a farmer and grew wheat and potatoes on his forty-acre farm.

Betty was almost as wide as she was tall. A smiling, motherly woman with tremendous energy, she kept pigs and chickens and helped out with the arable work whenever it needed more hands. She was also the mother of two red-headed sons who ran wild a lot of the time, but helped with the farm work when needed.

Betty arrived on our doorstep the day after we moved in with a basket of eggs, telling Mum whenever we needed eggs we could have some. Her hens always produced more than she could sell locally. Mum and Betty became instant friends. Both good practical cooks and domestic managers, they had a similar outlook and their friendship lasted for life. Dad and Geoff got on well too and before the week was out they were travelling together each morning to High Wycombe to get the train to London.

We had only been in the house a few days when I received the dreadful news that I would be starting at the local school the following Monday. Visions of the nuns I had been so happy to leave behind gave me bad dreams that night, but there was no escaping the inevitable. The only saving grace was that Rodney Copping, Betty's younger son, would be going with me. Language was a still a bit of a problem because although my English had improved, it was still far from fluent. But Rodney was an outdoors, practical sort of boy and it only took seconds to determine that we were kindred spirits, with common skills and interests. Our mothers took it in turns to deliver us each morning to the village school, dressed up like trussed turkeys in grey shorts and jackets, with silly school caps crammed on our heads.

I managed to cause chaos the first morning by releasing a mouse I had caught in the woods behind our house. As it scuttled across the floor, one of the girls saw it and screamed, leaping onto her chair. In seconds the place was in uproar. Rodney and I made a play of trying to catch the beast, while the rest of the class, including the teacher, climbed onto chairs and desks in case it ran up their legs.

This was almost as much fun as Gilbert, Robert and I used to have nun-baiting.

The row this incident caused brought the head teacher, who was not amused. She soon restored order. It must have been the fact that we thought it was funny that identified Rodney and me as the culprits, earning us whacked knuckles from the teacher's ruler and half an hour standing in the corridor facing the wall until the lesson ended.

Two days later, we brought a slow worm to school, with similar results. This earned us a reprimand in the head teacher's study and we were held inside after school until the collecting parent came in search of us. It was Betty who came that day, listened to the teacher's protests about our behaviour and promised to pass on the message to my mother. When we got out to her car, she almost wet herself laughing as we confessed what we'd done, and never bothered to tell us off. Rodney and I stood outside the window and listened when she told Mum, and we could hear the two of them giggling. All the same, they both managed to keep straight faces when we came inside in search of tea and cake.

My mother had long ago got used to me bringing in beasties I had caught in the bush and, provided I didn't let them loose in her kitchen or bring them to the table at mealtimes, she never complained as long as I wasn't cruel to my captives.

School was boring and I didn't learn much there, but before long, spring arrived and the countryside woke up. This offered limitless interest and also, on my birthday, a bicycle. It was second-hand, painted bright green, and had new tyres but no gears –

they were for posh bikes. Going around the green and up and down the farm lane, it took me four days to master the art of not falling off, after which the surrounding lanes became my playground. Rodney also had a bike so we explored together. He'd been born there, so he already knew his way around, but together we were able to extend our range, first as far as the mushroom farm, a mile along the road, and then further afield.

A few miles away there was an RAF airfield, where fighter jets regularly took off and landed. We could often be found sitting on the grass at the end of the runway, our bikes dumped in the hedge, watching Gloster Meteors roaring overhead as they clawed their way aloft. There was also a Mosquito squadron at Bovingdon and we occasionally saw them take off in pairs. With their sleek lines and the deep throaty grumble of their engines, they were far more exciting than the roaring, screaming jets, and yet we recognised the latter represented the future. Rodney had never been in a plane, but the memory of the flight from Lusaka and my visit to the cockpit gave us plenty to talk and dream about.

We'd also discovered Biggles books. Rodney received two for his birthday, and he read them aloud to me.

As summer approached, the Coppings called for help to get their crop of new potatoes out of the ground. We all went down the lane to howk tatties. Geoff was an inventive engineer and had cannibalised several old farm machines, some dating from the Edwardian era, adapting the pieces to work behind his small grey Ferguson tractor. Now he could drive along the rows while a whirling, spinning monster behind churned up the soil, spraying out stones and potatoes to lie on the surface. People following behind would then collect the crop in sacks, leaving full bags dotted across the field in their wake. Once all the tatties had been

A Gloster Meteor fighter taking off from RAF Bovingdon.

howked out of the ground, Geoff replaced the machine with a trailer to collect the full sacks. It was backbreaking work, but great fun, and when it was done Betty fed everyone well.

At the end of the day, we received a big bag of new spuds to take home with us, as payment for our labour. We'd have done it for nothing because the Coppings were our friends, but times were still tight in post-war Britain and we weren't going to refuse this free food.

The day after the tattie howking I went down the lane to find Rodney, hoping he would be interested in cycling over to watch the jets. He was not at home, but his mum was. When I asked where he was, she pointed out to the fields. "Somewhere down there. He's ploughing the nine acre," she said.

Sure enough, at the bottom of the field I found my friend, only just seven years old, seated atop the grumbling grey tractor, ploughing beautifully straight furrows across the field where the previous day we'd been bagging potatoes. He stopped to let me climb up beside him and we spent the rest of the afternoon together, going up and down the field. At tea time, his elder brother, Jeremy, came and took over to finish the field. Rodney had already done more than half of it.

WE NEEDED A CAR at Lye Green, so Dad bought a dark green fourteen-horsepower Wolseley, with leather bench seats and windows that always misted up in cold weather. Soon after we'd arrived Mum learned that if she wanted to drive in Britain, she'd have to pass a driving test. This seemed a bit daft as she'd been driving for years, having driven ambulances, trucks and buses in India all through the war, and she'd driven our old Ford all over Northern Rhodesia, and never had an accident. But rules are rules, so she had to take a test.

The test centre was in High Wycombe, a small town nestling in a deep valley, with a long steep hill on each side of it. Inevitably, the test centre was down in the town centre and the test route included a trip up and down at least one of the hills. Since High Wycombe was some miles away from Lye Green and had bigger shops than Chesham, Mum decided it would be a good place to buy new shoes for me, as my feet were difficult to fit and there might be more choice there. She blamed too many years running around the African bush with no shoes on for spreading my feet so that even the widest fittings were often too narrow. Not wanting to waste the opportunity, she decided to combine a shopping trip with the driving test.

The test examiner said it was a bit irregular having a passenger in the car during the test, but eventually gave up arguing when Mum said he'd have to provide someone to look after me if I couldn't come too. He glared at me and told me I'd have to sit still and say nothing. Then he climbed into the car and slammed the door far harder than necessary.

Traffic was light through the town and Mum had no problem manoeuvring the heavy car round the streets. The examiner asked her to go up one of the hills and halfway up, he made her do an emergency stop. She had no trouble, but I saw the evil grin on his face as he told her to carry on up the hill. He obviously thought starting on the hill would defeat her, but she wasn't going to be beaten and set off like a professional. She started so smoothly he made her stop again, just where the hill was steepest. Again she had no trouble and he looked almost disappointed. Then he told her to do a three-point turn on the hill.

Mum must have guessed he was being deliberately difficult. Clearly he didn't want this pretty, capable woman to pass the test, and was looking for an excuse to fail her. This didn't bother Mum and she made the move with ease. Not to be defeated, the examiner made her do another emergency stop going downhill and then repeat the three-point turn. When she did all these manoeuvres correctly, he gave up and told her to take him back to the test centre.

As he handed her a pink form and said she'd passed, he told her she ought to think about becoming a driving instructor. Her test was the best piece of driving he'd seen since he became an examiner.

We forgot about shoe shopping and Mum sang all the way home.

One Saturday morning, after a hard week in stuffy London offices, Dad decided get some fresh air and went outside to cut logs for the fire. There were a number of fallen trees in our wood so, after he and I had dragged a selection of large branches closer to the back of the house, he got out his bow saw and fitted a new blade. Five minutes later, he came in with his left hand covered in blood. The blade had slipped and he'd almost sliced his thumb off. Mum immediately put a tourniquet round his arm and wrapped his hand in a clean tea towel. She took the ice tray from the small freezer compartment in the fridge and wrapped all the ice cubes in another tea towel, strapping this round the first one which was already turning red with the seeping blood. Telling me to look after the house, she piled Dad into the car and set off for the hospital in Amersham.

A few minutes later, Betty turned up to ask Mum something, but went away when she heard what had happened, saying she'd send Rodney up the lane to keep me company. When he arrived, I was cleaning the blood off Dad's bow saw, thinking it wouldn't get used for a while if his hand was no use. He'd cut his left hand – the same one German shrapnel had already reduced to only half a hand during the war.

Rodney suggested we should carry on where he'd left off. He regularly used a bow saw on the farm, so while I held the wood, he sawed, and we soon reduced the fallen tree to usable logs. After he'd finished, I wanted to have a go, so we got another fallen branch from the woods and started on that. By the time Mum and Dad came back from the hospital, four hours later, we'd cut up most of the fallen branches and had made a huge stack of logs beside the back door.

We earned our cake that afternoon.

21 ~ Return to Scotland

NOTHING LASTS FOREVER AND before we had been in Lye Green a year, Dad received another posting, this time to Scotland. He was going back to his own regiment, the Highland Light Infantry, to command a small depot in Glasgow. Out of the shed came the boxes Mum had so recently unpacked and our household disappeared into them again. In a matter of weeks, we were heading north to an army quarter at Thornliebank, on the outskirts of the city, in Giffnock.

A new home meant a new school, and I was enrolled in the junior section of Glasgow Academy. Alistair was still at his boarding school in Fife, and still hating it. The first time he came home for school holidays, he disappeared every morning and spent all day away from home. This carried on for almost two weeks before he was brought home by a burly official from nearby Rouken Glen Park. It seemed the council objected to his fishing in the park's lake and catching their pretty golden carp. The fact that he always put his catches back didn't matter: fishing there was forbidden.

A new school meant a new uniform, but fortunately in the junior school the rules were a little more relaxed. Most boys wore grey trousers with a school blazer, but this being Scotland, kilts were also acceptable. Money was still tight and a new school uniform was an unjustifiable burden since, although I was unaware of it, my parents were considering sending both Alistair and me to a boarding school in the south of England, where we'd both be needing another new uniform. Happily, since I already wore a kilt regularly, all Mum needed to buy for me was a second-hand blazer.

From the start of term, I walked up the road with my Dad each morning, me in my new uniform, Dad in his army kilt, to the corner of Rouken Glen Park. There we caught the tram into the city together.

The tram fare was ninepence and, since I usually offered a shilling, I got threepence change. At that time we still used 'proper money' in Scotland and the three-penny piece was a small silver coin, much prettier than the large multi-faceted brass thing used in England. I started saving these and in a few months amassed a reasonable collection. Many years later, I turned eight of them into a bracelet for my wife, Gay; she wears it every day.

Most of the streets in Glasgow city centre were cobbled, which made driving along them, or riding a bicycle, quite uncomfortable. To add to the hazards for cyclists, most streets had at least one set of tramlines going down the middle. The bigger roads had trams going in both directions. Catching a bicycle wheel in the tramline could tip you off in seconds and, because the trams were electric, they didn't make much noise to warn you if you were about to be run over. Actually, it was only the newer trams that were quiet. We still had a number of the old 'bone shaker' models running on the less-frequented routes, including those out to the suburbs.

It was one of these bone shakers that Dad and I usually caught

Trams were an efficient form of urban transport, particularly on the cobbled streets of Glasgow.

each morning. In addition to being rickety and noisy, they were very draughty and cold in inclement weather, which meant most of the time as many of them had windows missing and there was no door at the back where we got on and off. The newer models were more streamlined and almost comfortable.

Old or new, the trams all ran on time and you never had to wait more than a few minutes for one, even during quieter parts of the day.

School was no fun. We were confined to either the dingy cold classrooms or to an asphalt-covered playground from eight-thirty in the morning until four in the afternoons, five days a week. I longed for the freedom of the African bush, for the bugs and beetles, the snakes and *chongololos*, and most of all for my African friends. I got to know my new classmates, but none of them ever qualified as friends in the way Gilbert, Robert and Nasouma had been. Here, we never saw one another outside school, even though a few lived quite close to us in Thornliebank.

170 • WILD CHILD

Dad took us up to Loch Lomond and Loch Katryn on Sunday expeditions. I liked the wildness of the Trossachs countryside, but it still lacked something.

When summer came, he took us on a long-promised camping trip in the islands. He borrowed a tent big enough for all four of us from the army store and put a roof rack on the car to carry it. Our luggage and gear filled the boot and back of the car, leaving just enough room for my brother and me to squeeze in. Mum had started learning to paint in oils, so her easel was strapped to the roof with the tent and Alistair's fishing rods. A box of paint and brushes took its place on the back seat between my brother and me, while Mum and Dad had the food box between them in the front.

It seemed to take hours to get anywhere; we had to drive almost up to Oban and the roads up there were narrow and winding, often single tracks with passing places. To relieve the boredom, we played games like I-Spy. When we ran out of ideas for games, my brother and I drove our parents mad singing advertising jingles we'd heard on the radio. There was one particularly irritating jingle for cat food which we repeated many hundreds of times. It had a certain rhythm to it which we felt somehow diminished the miles, if not the boredom.

"Isn't it a pity that all kittens don't get Kit-e-Kat."

Repeat that to yourself half a dozen times in quick succession and you'll see what I mean. You'll also remember it for at least the rest of the day, if not for life. I have!

An hour or so after Inverary, we came to a small hump-backed bridge. At that time, Clachan Bridge was the only bridge joining any of the Hebridean islands either to the mainland or to each other. A spur from the Atlantic washed right in here around Seil Island, so this was known as the only bridge over the Atlantic. It

The car was so overloaded it couldn't get over the Clachan Bridge to Seil Island.

had been built in the 1790s so slate from a quarry on Seil could be brought to the mainland.

As we headed over the bridge, it became apparent that we had a problem. Our car grounded on the hump back and would go no further. It was quite a low slung car anyway, but the additional weight of the tent and all the camping gear, together with the four of us and our supplies was too much for the suspension. There was nothing for it but to unload, let Dad drive over, and then carry the baggage across. Fortunately, our destination was only a few yards beyond the bridge, but it still felt like a long walk after sitting in the car for hours.

Mrs McPherson, the owner of the field we were going to camp in, must have been on the lookout for us as she soon came waddling up the lane like a stumpy tartan penguin, to bid us welcome and to ask if we needed anything. She had fresh milk from her own cow, butter too, if we wanted it, along with eggs and some nice fresh fish her son had brought in not an hour earlier.

I asked her in Gaelic what sort of fish it was and immediately became her favourite person. She offered haddock, whiting or

Pitching the tent in Mrs McPherson's field on Seil Island.

mackerel and fresh oatmeal to coat it if we wanted to fry some.

"That's supper sorted!" said Mum with obvious delight. She walked with Mrs McPherson back to her cottage to collect supplies, and came back laden.

Hearing that her son was a fisherman brought Alistair to life and before she left, Mrs McPherson had promised him a fishing trip with her son in his boat. As a result of this, he was almost helpful when it came to putting up the tent. We chose a place sheltered by a dry stone wall.

Being an army tent, it had a fly sheet and far more poles than any tent we had used before. It took a while sorting out which one went where. Eventually we made sense of it and we got the thing more or less upright. There remained only the matter of banging pegs onto the rocky ground to secure all the guy ropes. This proved to be a far harder that it looked as the topsoil was so thin there was nothing to bang the pegs into. In the end, we had to tie at least half of the guy ropes to the biggest rocks we could bring up from the seashore, a hundred yards away. By the time we had finished erecting the tent, a cold, thin rain was falling. We were glad to get under cover.

Using a spare fly sheet, Dad rigged an awning to protect our cooking area and then set about lighting the primus stove to boil a kettle for tea. Dad sent Alistair off up the hill to fill a large water can with fresh spring water, saying it would taste much better than the Glasgow tap water we had brought with us, which smelled of chlorine.

Mum came back laden with eggs, milk, fish and a pile of shortbread the old lady had sent to me. Mum sad she'd been so delighted to be greeted in her native tongue she refused all payment for the supplies. A bit like Africa: that's how things worked in the highlands and islands.

The next morning, the sun was shining so we set out to explore the little island. The village consisted of only a few cottages and beyond them the road vanished, becoming no more than an overgrown track that went around the hill to a long-abandoned slate quarry. There was a small pier opposite the village, where coastal puffers used to dock in bygone years, with a breakwater and several small boats tied to moorings in its lee. A few more boats were upturned on the rocky shore, above the tide line, in various stages of repair and painting.

As we walked down to the shore, a tall red-haired man of about forty came over and introduced himself as Mrs McPherson's son, Andy. He'd already heard that Alistair was keen on fishing and offered to take him out on the afternoon tide. The offer didn't include me, but I didn't mind. There was plenty to do on the island and I was already engrossed in the myriad coloured sea urchins I had discovered clinging to the legs of the pier. The water was so clear it gave a grandstand view without getting wet. Limpets covered the rocks and their empty shells were strewn along the foreshore below our tent. Over the next few days, I spent hours scouring the beach for these shells, collecting as many as I could of the same size, intending to string them together to make Mum a necklace. I even prised a few from the rocks with my penknife.

In the end they never got made into a necklace. Adult limpet shells were tough, hard to remove from the rocks and even harder to bore holes in. The little ones I was collecting were much more fragile and it took me a while to learn both how to lift them cleanly, and how to bore holes in them without breaking the whole thing. Once I had patiently pierced each one, Mum attached them with crochet stitches all round the edge of a circular piece of mosquito netting to make what she called a *jaali*. This was a cover for jugs of milk or other liquids and it served to keep flies out. We had others at home, made with glass beads round the edge.

Ever practical and resourceful, Mum had learned to make these things in India (hence the name) and had produced a number of different-sized ones over the years, each one with a signifi-

The Seil Jaali still covers our water jug sixty years later.

cance of its own. This was going to be our *Seil jaali*. In all, she sewed on sixty-seven limpet shells with a glass bead in the centre of the net as a handle. Our *Seil jaali* is still in regular use, sixty years later.

Alistair had a great day out with Andy McPherson and came back with an invitation to go salmon fishing with him a few days later. They had caught plenty of fish and he proudly brought a large haddock home for supper. I was disappointed. I didn't really like fish and had been hoping for some of Mrs McPherson's mutton stew whose rich aroma I had smelled earlier. But Dad said this was Alistair's catch, so we would have it for supper and be grateful.

The next day, while Mum painted, Dad decided it was an ideal time to repay Mrs McPherson for her hospitality and all the produce she had given us. We would go up to *bac mòno* and bring the dried peats down to her cottage. While we were at it, we'd cut her another load and stack it to dry in the breeze. When he told us the old lady was almost eighty and still cut her own peats, any objections we might have been tempted to offer shrivelled on our tongues.

Dad must have spoken to Andy about this, for we found a stack of peat kreels inside the corner of our field in the morning, with a small map of how to find his family's part of *bac mòno* when we went up the hill to the moor. Dad told me to sneak down and bring the *sleaghdn* from Mrs McPherson's shed, and to try and do it without her seeing me. Easy.

It seemed like a long way up to the moor, but it only took about fifteen minutes to get to the right place. There were rows of dried peats stacked, leaning against one another with another on top to form little arches for the wind to blow through. Peat shrinks as it dries; the cut slabs were stacked this way to ensure that they dried evenly and didn't fall over as they shrank. The kreels held a surprising amount and were lighter than they looked when filled. I was still too small to carry a full one, but strong enough to slide one down the grassy, heather-clad slope and not let go. It took us five trips to bring down all that had already been cut and dried, and it was after lunchtime when we had finished.

Mum had made us a pile of sandwiches which we'd taken up the hill in the morning. When we got up there again after stacking the last load of dried peats behind the old lady's cottage, we sat on the bank in the sun and ate them, dirty, peaty hands notwithstanding. No food ever tasted so good.

After lunch, we tried our hands at cutting more peats. With his injured hand, Dad couldn't manage the lift and twist action very easily. Alistair had a go and made it look much easier. It required a little bit of strength to toss the wet peat up from the bottom of the bank, but it was more about balance. After he'd cut a row, it was my turn. I found it surprisingly easy. We left Dad on top of the bank stacking, while we took it in turns to cut and toss ten slabs each before changing places. By tea time, we'd cut and stacked two full rows – twice as much as we'd carried down to the cottage earlier. Dad declared it a good day's work and suitable payment for the old lady's generosity.

Alistair went fishing with Andy the following day and returned in the evening with a nine-pound salmon. He'd caught it on a fly Andy had given him. The catch fuelled his enthusiasm for fly-fishing and started an interest in tying his own flies that lasted many years and resulted in some beautiful and spectacular lures. When we got home, Mum insisted he got dressed up smartly to have his picture taken with the fish in our back garden.

All too soon our holiday came to an end and as we packed up, the rain began, making our heavy tent even heavier. We had to lug it, and everything else, along the road and over the bridge before loading the car.

As we were about to leave, Mrs McPherson arrived with a basket of goodies she'd baked that morning to sustain us on our journey. It included a slab of her special homemade tablet.

For those not familiar with traditional Scottish cooking and sweetmeats, tablet is a confection of butter and sugar boiled together until it crystalises. Mrs McPherson added a secret ingredient of her own, a peaty flavoured liquid produced in a small still she kept hidden in the bothy behind her cottage. She'd given Dad a few drams during our stay and he said it was very good. Totally illegal her whisky may have been, but it certainly made her tablet taste special.

Alistair with his first salmon.

22 ~ Aden and boarding school

WE HAD ONLY BEEN IN Glasgow eighteen months when Dad received another posting. It seemed the post in Scotland had been a temporary measure to keep him busy until the job the War Office really wanted him to do fell vacant. This time he was posted to Aden, as the Army member of a senior joint services planning team.

The move meant changing schools again. I couldn't stay where I was and there was no suitable school in Aden. Since the Army paid school fees while Dad was overseas, I would be going to a boarding school. Alistair meanwhile had always hated the school he was at in Fife, so our parents decided to send us both to Falconbury, a small preparatory boarding school in Sussex. We could join our family in Aden for the holidays.

Two days before the new term started, we all took the night train to London. We stayed overnight in a rather frayed hotel and the next day, dressed in new school uniforms, we went to Victoria station with our trunks to catch the school train. We met a few of the boys on it, but most of them already knew one another well, so we stood out as different. I got a thumping from one boy

Falconbury School, near Bexhill-on-Sea.

because he said he couldn't understand me. I later discovered he was the school bully and such thumpings happened a number of times over the first two terms, until I learned a lot more English and finally used my fists.

It didn't take long for me to decide I didn't like boarding school. I began to understand why Alistair had hated the one in Fife. Being crammed with about sixty other boys into a large red-brick building, shrouded in Virginia creeper was not fun.

The school was half a mile from the sea. Behind it were large playing fields stretching down to a two-acre vegetable plot which supplied all the fruit and vegetables we ate. Once discovered, the vegetable plot made a good place to escape to. I did as often as I could, always making sure the gardener didn't see me. He was very protective about his domain and didn't want little boys messing about in there, pinching his beans. I got my ear twisted several times when I failed to pay attention and got caught helping myself to pods from the plants or pulling up juicy fresh carrots.

At the end of the year, Alistair left Falconbury and moved on to a senior school in Dorset, leaving me a pile of second-hand uniform that I was rapidly growing into. We hadn't seen much of one another in term time, because he was in the top class and I was in the bottom one, although I knew he was around. Now, with him gone, it became apparent that he'd been covering my back all the time. The school bully, who had thumped me that day on the school train, decided this was his opportunity to have another go at me, and at another lad called Tony. He would regularly beat up one or other of us in the changing rooms when we came in from the games field.

One day when I came in soaking wet after a football game, he was in the drying room punching Tony. The drying room was about fifteen feet long and eight feet wide with a row of pegs all round the wall for hanging up wet clothing. Around the bottom of the wall ran two large steam pipes, too hot to touch, which kept the room hot enough to dry out our sopping sports gear. Hearing Tony's cries, I went in and found the bully kicking and punching him. When he saw me, he turned to have a go at me, but I moved faster than him. Grabbing him by the waistband of his shorts, I lifted him bodily onto the row of hooks and left him hanging there. Putting his feet on the heating pipes, he tried to stand and lever himself off the hooks, so I grabbed his feet, undid his laces, and pulled off his football boots and socks. When he put his bare feet on the hot pipes he rapidly lifted them off and screamed blue murder. I pulled Tony out into the changing room and shut the door.

One of the staff must have heard the noise as the games master soon appeared to find out what was going on. Though muffled, the bully's screams were still audible, despite the general hubbub of the changing room, so he went in to rescue him. Having released the boy from the hooks, the master emerged with a smile on his face to enquire who had put him there. I owned up.

"Why did you do it?" he asked.

"He's been thumping me at every opportunity, and today he was kicking the shit out of Tony," I replied.

I never saw the hand that whacked me round the ears, but I saw plenty of stars.

"Don't you dare use language like that!" the master roared.

"Why? It's what everyone else says. What's wrong with it?"

"Don't be impertinent, boy. You'll see the headmaster this evening."

That meant I would get thrashed with a cane. Seeing the headmaster always meant that.

He waited while we all got changed and dispersed to our classrooms.

Back in my own class, the other boys looked at me differently. Most of them had only tolerated me before, because I was different and my English was still poor. There were two boys whose parents lived in East Africa and who spoke a bit of Chinyanja, so at least I had someone who understood why I was different and why my English was so poor. But this afternoon's events had changed all that. I had taken on the school bully and won. This earned me a measure of respect, both for doing that and for the caning I was going to get later.

Seeing the headmaster always took place after we'd all gone to bed. The master who had ordered the punishment came to the dormitory before lights out and escorted me down to the headmaster's study, leaving me outside the door, and merely knocking to let him know I was there.

A few moments later the door opened. The headmaster, Philip Devitt, was a thin balding man with a military bearing. He ushered me inside and then sat down at his desk, asking me to explain what had happened earlier. I told him how the bully had been picking on me and Tony since the first day on the school train. I told him about the times I found my ankle being kicked or my hand stood on deliberately during games, and I told him what had happened when I found him kicking Tony after games.

He then asked what I had said to the games master, and I repeated what I'd said. He looked slightly startled, but made no comment for a moment. He patiently explained that certain words were very rude and should not be used. I asked which words and he recited a long list, many of which I had not previously heard.

"Please don't use any of those words in future," he said. "Now what are we going to do with you?"

"I suppose you're going to cane me, sir."

"No, I don't think that would do any good, do you?" he said, thoughtfully. "But from now on kindly don't hang anyone else up to dry. Matron doesn't like having to treat burned feet. And don't swear. I know your English isn't very good yet, but you're learning and I think you know the difference."

With that he asked me to stand aside, drew a cane out of the walking stick stand behind the door, making sure to rattle the bunch as he did so, and gave the upholstered arm of his armchair four hard whacks.

"Keep rubbing your backside and don't tell anyone," he said with a conspiratorial wink.

When I got back to my dormitory the lights were out. As I climbed into bed, whispered voices from across the room asked if it had hurt.

"Not much," I replied, and made sure to keep my backside away from anyone's view for the next few days, in case the lack of stripes on my buttocks gave the secret away.

LESSONS WEREN'T MUCH fun, except for French, because I could already understand quite a lot and the French master thought I was worth encouraging. I started to learn the piano, but after the first year, our music teacher left to become a concert pianist in South Africa. He was replaced by Miss Stein, a woman with a hooked nose, hairy arms and a pink plastic ruler with which she would rap my knuckles if I made a mistake. One day she did it once too often. After the fifth or sixth time, she drew blood. I snatched the ruler from her hands, snapped it in half, threw it on the floor and walked out. It was the first but definitely not the last time that I would stand up to an attacker and put their weapon out of action.

That night of course I had to go and see the headmaster again. I'm not sure it was my blooded knuckles that saved me from the cane this time, or the fact that he'd beaten me two days before for pinching broad beans from the kitchen garden and my backside was still striped and tender. In any event, Miss Stein wasn't allowed near a ruler again. She left at the end of that term and we were without a music teacher for several terms. By the time a new one arrived, I'd lost interest in the piano. I never had much musical talent anyway, so I didn't mind. I was unaware at the time how much of a disappointment this was to my Dad, but then I didn't know he'd played the piano and the saxophone in his youth, and had only stopped playing when his hand was blown apart. If I'd known that then, I might have made more effort to learn and play properly.

Boarding schools in Britain are a competitive environment in many ways, one of which manifested itself at the beginning of Lent. It seemed some sort of sacrifice was called for and boys were trying to outdo one another with things they thought up. I had a particularly sweet tooth as a youngster, so to give up sweets and sugar would be a challenge. Since I was in the habit of putting five spoonfuls of sugar in a half-pint mug of tea, refraining from this would indeed be a sacrifice. To take it a stage further, I elected also not to eat any sweets. At the time we were issued with one boiled sweet after lunch each day, so I put mine in a tin which I hid in the back of my school locker, dreaming of the sweet feast I could have when Easter finally arrived. Of course, this was rather missing the point of sacrifice, but I didn't understand that at the time.

When Easter arrived and I could resume eating sugary things, it was a bit of a let-down. The first sweet I put in my mouth tasted sickly, and I spat it out. Never mind, at least I could have sugar in my tea. Seated at the long table in the dining room, I was distracted by the boy to my left when the mugs of tea were being passed along and didn't notice that the boy to my right heaped a load of sugar into my mug before passing it to me. When the sugar bowl arrived, I tipped five spoonfuls into the mug and passed the bowl to my left. Then the boy to my right distracted me while the one on the other side also loaded sugar into my mug. When I stirred it myself, it felt thick. I marvelled at how, after a month without it, one could forget what stirring tea with sugar in felt like.

Schoolboys aged nine are disgusting creatures, so I took an enormous gulp of my tea. The taste was indescribably sickly. So much so, that I was promptly sick all over the table, splattering the boy opposite, and those on either side, amid an uproar of laughter from all those around me. Apart from the embarrassment this caused, I had to spend the next half hour cleaning up the mess and weeks being the subject of other boys' jibes. I never put sugar in tea again.

I was impatient for the end of term and another aeroplane

flight, this time to Aden. Nick Holmes, an old family friend who'd served with Dad in the Indian Army during the war, was delegated to collect Alistair and me from our school trains and deliver us to the aeroplane. Nick was a lovely man with a wonderful sense of humour. At the time, he worked for the BBC in London. He'd started as a radio newsreader because of his lovely voice, and eventually moved into management. He took us back to the BBC from the railway station, and parked us in the audience seats of a studio for an hour or so while he finished work. We stayed with his family for one or two nights before going to Heathrow to catch the plane to Aden.

The BOAC stewardesses were good at taking care of unaccompanied children. They gave us cardboard model aeroplanes to assemble, sweets to suck during climb and descent, and hot meals that tasted much better than school food. An indication that we were inter-

The control panel of a DC-4 Argonaut in which we flew to Aden. I was to come to know cockpits like this well years later, during the Biafran war.

ested in how the plane worked invariably got us invitations to the flight deck, where the crew were happy to explain things.

An invitation to the cockpit was as fascinating as it had been the first time I flew out of Lusaka. This plane looked a lot more complicated, but was just as exciting. The roof of the cockpit, as well as the instrument panel, was covered with dials and switches, but the magic of what all the dials and lights displayed was just as intense.

Travelling to Aden, we usually flew in either a Douglas DC-6 Argonaut or a Bristol Britannia. Both types had four engines, but the first had a bulbous nose and big radial engines that grumbled and snarled, emitting huge clouds of black smoke when they started. The Britannia, by contrast, was sleek and streamlined. It had turboprop engines which had a distinct whistle, earning it the name of the Whispering Giant. The Britannia wasn't exactly quiet, simply less noisy than the Argonaut.

Air travel was a pleasure as well as a fast and reasonably reliable means of going places. A journey of any distance was made up of a series of short hops. Occasionally aircraft broke down, meaning we had to wait a few hours before continuing. The crew knew just what to do in such events and either took us to an airport lounge and plied us with food and drink or, in extreme cases, transferred us to a local hotel to wait in comfort (at no cost to us) until the plane was repaired or replaced. We certainly weren't treated like 'self-loading cargo' as passengers are so often today.

The flights to Aden always stopped twice. The first stop was usually in Rome or Athens, where passengers waited in a transit lounge for an hour while ground crew refuelled the plane and cleaned the cabin before it flew on to Khartoum. I'll never forget landing in Khartoum and catching the first scent of Africa on the warm air when the cabin crew opened the door. It felt like a welcoming embrace. Never mind that we often had to wait two hours in Khartoum; this always felt as if I'd come home.

At Aden, our plane circled the old volcano with the port laid out below us. We could see ships at anchor and the white wakes that betrayed the bustle of small boats going about their business.

But where Khartoum had felt warm and welcoming, this desert outpost was alien. A wave of searing hot air flowed in when the aircraft door was opened. It was a shock after the air-conditioned comfort in which we'd travelled. Intense heat deflected off the bare concrete as we walked to the terminal, and yet it was still only 9.30 in the morning.

Our home in Aden was on the top floor of a small four-storey block in the crater. It overlooked a hockey ground, beyond which was one of the palaces belonging to the Sultan of Lahej. This sprawling complex was his town house, his main palace being about twenty miles away in the hills of Lahej itself. As well as being a traditional chieftain, the sultan was a modern businessman. Among his many business interests were a fleet of small fishing boats and two bottling plants, one producing only Coca Cola, the other produced drinks such as Tango, Stim and 7Up. He was far from reclusive, unlike some other Arab rulers, and interacted fluently with the Europeans in the colony.

Not long after Alistair and I arrived for our first visit, he invited us to tour of one of his factories and see the bottles which were sold on every street corner in the bazaar being filled. The plant was a bright, noisy place, with lines of glistening, clear bottles marching along tortuous conveyors, filled suddenly with colour, capped, turned over to make sure they didn't leak, and then stacked in crates by a team of sweating men. It was hot and noisy inside because of all the machinery, but to add to the cacophony, Arabic music blared from loudspeakers throughout the building. The music stopped only at prayer time, when the *muezzin's* call replaced the music and the plant paused for fifteen minutes to allow the workers to observe their devotions. Not all of them prayed, but most took the opportunity to sluice cold water over themselves, wash off the sweat, and rest for a few moments. As soon as the prayers were over, the music resumed and production began again.

Aden had grown around the remains of the extinct volcano. One edge of the crater had collapsed into the sea in antiquity. Long before the modern outer harbour had been constructed, the shoreline had been developed into a bustling waterfront, used by fishermen and small local trading boats. It was only a short walk from our house to the sea. We regularly saw fishermen walking up from the shore, past our building on their way to the bazaar, many carrying baskets of colourful freshly landed fish. Some brought hammerhead sharks and other denizens of the deep. The sharks were often bigger than the wiry little fishermen, who would hook the strange hammer-like head over their shoulder, leaving the tail to drag behind them on the ground. Invariably a procession of hungry pie dogs that populated our part of the crater followed them.

There was one particular pie dog we named Patch, because of a strange rectangular white mark on his rump. He often slept in the shade of our car when it was parked outside the block, and I took to dropping him morsels of food from our balcony. It didn't take long to make friends with Patch, who responded eagerly to any gesture of kindness, although everyone advised me to be careful and have nothing to do with pie dogs as they carried rabies.

Although I had heard all about rabies in Africa, I had never seen its effects and so was not deterred. He might not have been a domesticated dog, but by my reasoning he was much less of a risk than many of the animals I had been used to handling in the bush, and he was my friend. Whenever I appeared, Patch would come trotting over to see me, his tail wagging vigorously even if I wasn't offering food. Most of the Europeans, and all of our Arab neighbours, found this disconcerting.

Crater was a bustling, noisy place where there was always something interesting to see from the balcony on top of our block. It was even more interesting on the ground, with three long bazaar streets that we soon got to know well. It only took two days for Alistair to find a good fishing tackle shop which offered a vast variety of rods, reels, lines and lures at ridiculously cheap prices. Mum was with him when he discovered the shop and, finding the owner was an Indian, she addressed him in Urdu. They had such a long chat that Alistair finally had to interrupt to buy the tackle he wanted.

We got to know Sanjeev the shopkeeper very well. He was so pleased at finding a customer who could speak his language fluently that he gave us an additional massive discount that guaranteed him our custom whenever Alistair needed new fishing tackle. He also proved to be a good contact for Mum as he could usually introduce someone for anything she wanted in the bazaar. She quickly became well-known by the bazaar traders not only because of her ability to speak Urdu, but for her willingness to stop and chat and drink *chai*. She soon knew all the Indian tailors and could get new clothes for any of the family run up very cheaply, almost overnight, whenever we needed them.

Alistair took every opportunity he could to go fishing. He caught all manner of pretty fish and some quite large ones too. His biggest was a twenty-nine-pound shark, which took him more than fifteen minutes to bring ashore and prompted the purchase of a new rod and reel, with stronger line. I wasn't nearly as proficient as him. I only ever caught small sand sharks and stingrays, which would flap around waving their whip-like tails, trying to spike us with their stings. The difficult bit was turning it on its back and hold it steady enough to extract the hook from its mouth.

Fishing never held my interest for long anyway. I was more interested in scrambling up the rocky sides of the crater and exploring the mountain. I found a lot of interesting wildlife and small desert plants up there. It also gave a great view of the harbour and the airfield. Khormaksar served as both an RAF station and the civil airport, and was busy with the comings and goings of interesting aircraft. This was 1959, long before the troubles, when the garrison and the airfield became somewhat beleaguered outposts of the Empire.

At weekends, we spent most of our time beside the sea at Goldmohur beach. Facing out to sea with a backdrop of jagged, bare volcanic rock, the beach had a shark net hung in the water between two small promontories to keep swimmers safe. There was a small clubhouse and restaurant, and a saltwater swimming pool had recently been built. It was there that I managed to get my only significant case of sunburn.

There wasn't much to do down at the beach except swim or lie in the sun. A fence prevented me from exploring the surrounding mountainside, so I decided to try fishing from the rocks beyond the shark net. There I met a young Arab boy and, despite our lack of a common language, we managed to get along well. He was called Suleiman and he showed me the best place to cast my line. I later learned that his father was the caretaker of the beach and the clubhouse.

Suleiman and I sat in the sun all day fishing, wearing nothing more than swimming trunks, and occasionally dipping into the water for a few minutes to cool off. Nobody knew about sun block creams in those days, and all the lotions available were designed to increase tanning, not reduce it. By the time I was called to go home, I was well and truly roasted. I had long ago lost my African suntan but now my British pallor had turned an elegant shade of lobster pink, and my skin felt hot all over.

By sunset, my back felt like it was on fire, and it was beginning to blister. I lay on my belly and Mum covered me in calamine lotion. This soothed for a few moments while it was being applied, but the effect didn't last long. When our Yemeni cook, Ahmed, came in from the market with fresh vegetables for supper, Mum had a long conversation with him. Then she took over cooking the supper while Ahmed returned to the market in search of the ingredients for a concoction he assured her would sooth and heal my back. He returned half an hour later with an assortment of herbs and powders and began making something in the kitchen. It smelled totally diabolical and, with memories of some of the disgusting things the *ngangas* had made me drink in Rhodesia, I began to fear he was going to ask me to drink it. If he did, the cure would very definitely be worse than the ailment.

In the event, Ahmed's potion wasn't for drinking; it was a salve which he slathered all over my back, but before he did that, Ahmed gave me three large glasses of cold water to drink, ensuring that I wouldn't become dehydrated when he punctured and drained the huge blister which covered most of my back. I could feel the liquid from the blister dribbling down my flanks as he poked it with a table fork, and slowly the fire on my back diminished. When he had drained everything and applied his evil-smelling goo, he covered my back with a wet tea towel and told me to lie face down. He stayed all night, sitting by my bed, periodically replacing the goo and the wet tea towel and occasionally giving me more water to drink. By morning, the pain had gone.

Ahmed's treatment continued until lunchtime, when he expressed himself satisfied and told me to go and shower. I was alarmed to see that the water ran green, with lurid dark streaks in it, but there was no mirror in which I could see what my back liked like. There was no need for a towel as three minutes in the hot air on our balcony dried my skin. Ahmed told me not to wear a shirt for two days, and to stay in the shade. To everyone's amazement, after the two days, my back showed no sign of the blister and the skin was an even light brown all over.

Ahmed never disclosed what was in his concoction, but it certainly worked. Curiously, ever since then, my skin has tanned relatively easily, and never really burned, even without sun cream, which was a good thing as I later spent many years working in the tropical sun, usually wearing little more than a pair of shorts.

We made a few trips into the hinterland from Aden, with one particular trip to Lahej. Mum had been invited with June Knox-Mawer, the wife of Aden's Chief Justice, to visit the sultan's harem. I went to the palace with them and while they went into the harem to meet the sultan's women, I was taken on a tour of his stables and allowed to ride one of his horses. It was there that I had my first real encounter with a camel, which I was also allowed to ride. The sultan was proud of his camels, and entered them in the races held at the Aden Jockey Club. Dad liked horse racing, but never wagered large sums. He only ever had a small bet for the sake of interest. Having learned a little about gambling from the Chinese women in Penang, I knew all too well how fast you could lose everything, so I had effectively been warned off. I did, however, flutter a few shillings on the sultan's camels each time we went to the races – and several times I won twenty-five pounds or more.

Where we lived was separated from the main commercial port and administrative areas of Aden by the volcanic wall. A man-made cut provided a gateway, which was topped by a high arched bridge with high stone battlements on either side. Without going a long way round the coastal road, this was the only access. The sultan's Coca-Cola bottling plant was just inside the gate on the left.

A high fortified bridge topped Crater Gate.

On the other side of the road, between two windowless buildings a few yards down from the bottling plant, rough steps had been hacked into the rock. These led up inside the battlement to a path that wound its way up the crater wall, sometimes disappearing in a jumble of fallen basalt as it climbed the lower slopes of Jebel Shamsan, the highest peak in the crater rim. It was a four or five-hour hike to the top that had you scrambling over fallen slabs the size of a house, sometimes inching along ledges barely a handspan wide. It was hard climbing, but worth the effort as the views from the top were wonderful – provided the air was clear. All too often it was full of wind-blown dust, so anything beyond the crater was obscured by haze. On such days, the airfield at Khormaksar and the oil refinery at Little Aden, both of which were at sea level, were lost in the murk.

It was said that if you climbed Jebel Shamsan, you would never come back to Aden. I climbed it on each of the four school holidays I spent there, and was disappointed each time it failed to deliver its promise. Aden was fun for a visit, but I didn't really want to spend long there. While the people were nice, they lacked the warm vibrancy of Africans. Without the sea, Aden was a stark, monochrome place and no substitute for the African bush.

I wanted to be back in Africa.

After eighteen months I got my wish. Dad was promoted to Lieutenant Colonel and posted to command the training depot of the soon-to-be-independent Nigerian army at Zaria, in the northern region.

We moved back to Britain, where Mum and Dad stayed in a borrowed house in Berkhamstead. The old War Office had become the Ministry of Defence and, after two months' leave, Dad went to London each day to be briefed on his new assignment, before moving to Nigeria in August 1960, ahead of its independence on 1 October.

THAT YEAR, DURING the Easter holidays, Mum's youngest brother Freddie came to visit us in Berkhamstread and stayed a week. The Royal Ballet, with whom he was a dancer in the chorus, was about to embark on a tour of Scandinavia and he had a few days off before departure.

Freddie was charming and I wished we'd more time to get to know him properly. Although I asked, he never explained the rift that had torn Mum's family apart and kept them distant from us. All he did tell me was that his father had been a cantankerous old devil with a liking for the bottle and a temper that would have made a Scottish wildcat look placid. He had been thrashed regularly by his father when he was small, and because of that, he'd run away when he was fourteen and joined the ballet. Besides being a dancer, Freddie was also responsible for scenery and props, and helped with make-up. Like Mum, Freddie had very nimble fingers. In his spare time, such as he got, he liked mending clocks. Dad's old alarm clock, which had been prone to going off at unexpected times, worked perfectly after Freddie fixed it. He told me he also repaired dancers' shoes when they split and had considered becoming a shoemaker when his dancing days were over.

With the innocence of youth, one morning over breakfast I asked Freddie if he was queer. Mum was outraged and embarrassed, saying I shouldn't ask people questions like that, although the look on her face told me she had asked herself the same question. Freddie just grinned and asked what had prompted the question.

"One of the boys said all ballet dancers are queer," I replied.

"Well, some of them are, "Freddie laughed, "but don't suggest that to Alice or she'll knock you into next week."

"Who's Alice?" I asked.

"My girlfriend," he chuckled. "She's got a right hook like Don Cockell."

"I've met him," I said, "his son goes to my school."

"Well she's not as muscular as him, but packs the same punch."

Mum was clearly interested and asked about Alice. We learned that she was another dancer who had failed to get into the touring company because she was two inches too short. The Royal Ballet was very particular that all their dancing girls should be the same size. Freddie himself only made the grade by half an inch. Alice had a non-dancing job, but still trained with all the other dancers to fill in gaps in formations and keep herself fit.

"So are you going to marry her?" I asked.

"In the autumn, after we come back from Sweden," Freddie said. "That was one of my reasons for coming to visit. I wanted to ask if you'd all come to the wedding. I wanted to bring Alice to meet you, but she's gone to see her sick dad in Lincoln this week."

We never did get to their wedding, and nor did they. Mum and Dad were in Nigeria by the time the Royal Ballet returned from Scandinavia and in late November received a sad letter from Freddie saying that Alice had caught pneumonia in Sweden and died soon after they came home. Freddie withdrew after that and, although he carried on working for the Royal Ballet, only danced one more season. He occasionally wrote to Mum, but we never saw him again.

THAT SUMMER I HAD managed to scrape through the Common Entrance exam and so would be following my brother to a new school in Dorset in the autumn. I'd hated all the time I'd spent at boarding school in Sussex, and even the end of my final term had been traumatic.

I had found a snake in the long grass beside the sports field earlier in the term, so I coiled it up and kept it in my pocket in a silk bag. This was not before I'd opened its mouth and removed its fangs with my penknife. Each week I would sneak out of school, during free time on Saturday, and go down to the village pet shop where I bought the fattest white mouse I could for a penny. That was food for my snake. When it wasn't in my pocket, the snake lived in a glass tank on the window ledge in the school hobbies room, where it could bask in the sun. The staff knew I had got it but, provided I didn't play with it in class, took no notice and never examined it closely, assuming that it was harmless.

At the end of term, I was being collected by another boy's parents. They had also been in Northern Rhodesia. They were to deliver me to Nick Holmes's house, which was near where they now lived. As we were about to get into their car, Michael announced in a loud voice that I had a snake in my pocket.

"Don't be silly, Michael," his dad said. "People don't put snakes in their pockets."

"But he has! He has!" Michael insisted.

"Have you?" His dad enquired, turning to me.

"Yes, sir," I answered truthfully.

"Well let's see it then."

So I got out the silk bag, untied the string and tipped my fat and dozy snake into my hand, holding it forward for him to see.

Michael's dad took one brief glance and leapt back. "That's poisonous! Put it in the long grass immediately."

"Oh, it's quite safe, I've removed its fangs," I protested.

"That's as maybe. It's still a poisonous snake and it's not coming in my car!" He sounded frightened.

My protests fell on deaf ears. He was absolutely adamant and I had no choice but to put the snake in the long grass and let it go, wondering where it would find another white mouse next week. It was a good thing I had fed it that morning. At least that would keep it going until its fangs grew back.

I never forgave Michael or his dad for that, and was glad we wouldn't be going to the same school next term. I sat in the car and sulked, staring out the window, refusing to speak to anyone until we reached the Holmes's house.

23 ~ Nigeria and a change of school

MUM HAD SPENT A WEEK sorting out school clothing, replacing Alistair's nametapes with mine in the uniform he'd outgrown. By the time Mum and Dad were ready to leave for Nigeria, our school trunks were well on their way to Dorset. Mum and Dad drove Alistair and me over to Mortimer to spend our last week of summer holiday with the Holmes family, and then they flew to Kano.

At the beginning of term, we caught the school train down to Dorset. When we reached the school, Alistair showed me where my common room was, and how to find my dormitory. Then he vanished and I didn't see him for four days.

I hated the new school as much as I'd hated the last one, but at least here there were more opportunities to slope off on my own. Canford had 350 acres of grounds, much of it taken up by sports fields, but including some good wild areas with trees, scrub and ponds. It also had the River Stour flowing past the main school buildings, with a weir pool and a mill stream.

My dormitory was on the second floor, which meant I had to

Canford School in Dorset.

haul my trunk from the entrance up eighty-seven steps of a steep and narrow spiral staircase, against a constant stream of boys going the other way. Because I was a new boy, nobody offered to help and my brother was nowhere to be seen. It was only after I had been there a few weeks that I discovered there was a lift in the other tower. I could have taken the trunk up in that and then simply dragged it along a corridor. But new boys are never told about things like that and brotherly love had been subservient to school tradition, so he hadn't told me.

The culture was designed to humiliate those who didn't know the ropes, loading you with undignified and unnecessary tasks, making life difficult and ensuring you knew you were the lowest of the low. I was now a very small fish in a very big pond filled with predators. It was not unusual, in the first few weeks, to arrive in the dormitory at night to find my bed had been stripped and all my bedding was hanging out of the window on a bootlace. When I tried to rescue it, someone cut the bootlace and my bedding dropped. If I was lucky, it went right down to the ground, but sometimes it got hung up on a gargoyle or drain pipe, and would remain there until the school's maintenance men removed it a few days later. When this happened, it seemed inevitable that it was me who got punished, not whoever had hung the bedding out of the window and cut the bootlace. It was my bedding, so I was at fault.

On the second occasion this happened, I went down and found my bedding, took it to the bicycle sheds and slept there peacefully, returning everything to the dormitory while everyone else was having breakfast. The following evening, the three boys who had hung my stuff out the window found the legs of their pyjamas had been sewn up and when they got into their own beds, they each had a collection of frogs and toads waiting for them. One was so freaked out by this he took off down the corridor screaming and woke the whole place, bringing down the wrath of all the house prefects and our housemaster.

The talk around school the following day was quite amusing, but people treated me with a little more care after that. The established gang gave up trying to torment me since they realised I would not only retaliate, but do so in unconventional ways. Several woke up to find they had been tied by their ankles and wrists to the bedposts while they slept, and when they finally got free of that and tried to dress, the legs of their trousers had somehow been sewn up at the bottom, or they had earthworms in their socks which they never discovered until their toes encountered them.

I got to know a number of boys quite well, but the only one I would call a friend was Johnny McFarlane. Like me, he was singled out for being different, but in his case it was because he was a paraplegic. He'd had polio as an infant and wore leg irons and used crutches to get around. Bright and hard-working, he was streaks ahead of me academically, but we found all sorts of common interests and soon became firm friends. At some point, I christened him McDuff, and the name stuck. It has lasted a lifetime, along with our friendship and he became like another brother to me. This was hardly surprising since, despite being in different houses, I saw far more of him than I did of Alistair and over the years we shared many adventures and activities.

After three tedious months, the first term finally ended and we were off by air to Nigeria. Getting away from the school was like liberation from prison. A night flight across the Sahara landed us at Kano in time for an early breakfast. Looking out the window as we made our approach for landing, I was surprised to see two huge khaki-coloured pyramids, several hundred feet high. They were surrounded by housing, with a few heavy lorries and a lot of donkey carts parked on a nearby piece of open ground. I learned later that these pyramids were made with sacks of groundnuts, which was the main cash crop of the region.

When the aircraft door opened and the waft of warm air flowed in, I felt released. The smell of termites, dust, and all the familiar aromas of Africa offered a fanfare that let me feel really at ease for the first time in several years. Some people might think this fanciful, but anyone who has Africa in their soul will understand this.

Of course, Nigeria looked different from the parts of Africa that were most familiar to me, but at the same time it all looked right. Smiling black faces, bright-coloured clothing, parched red soils, dusty trees and scrub beside mud-walled buildings – even the scattering of rubbish that lined some urban streets all offered a sense of normality and lots of exciting potential.

The countryside round Kano was sparse and open, with few

A typical decorated house in northern Nigeria.

large trees and less organised agriculture than we had known in East Africa. The buildings had a style of their own, many having flat roofs with little ears sticking up at the corners. Most were unadorned, yet a few were painted white and some had their walls decorated with swirling knot patterns reminiscent of, but distinctly different from, the Celtic knot patterns that had been familiar in Scotland.

After breakfast, we headed south on the long road to Zaria. This was the middle of the short rainy season, so we took the winter road, which had a tarmac surface for the first thirty miles. After that it became a graded laterite strip, complete with the familiar corrugations, potholes and diversions where a culvert had collapsed or an aardvark had dug a hole. It was only 120 miles, but the trip took three and a half hours, so it was after lunchtime when we arrived.

The military cantonment was set on the edge of the Sabon Gari market area, a mile north of the old walled city. Like any old colonial military establishment, it was well set out, with mature trees shading many of the roadways, their trunks painted white up to waist level. The Commanding Officer's residence was the first house on the right inside the boundary fence. It had two gates to a large sweeping semi-circular drive lined with flowering hibiscus and poinsettia bushes, and an extensive garden in front of a white-painted thatched bungalow. There was another large garden behind the house in which, against all advice, my mother planted rose beds and bulbs. These produced a profusion of colourful and sweet-scented flowers all year long, earning the surprised admiration of all who saw them. She also planted a vegetable garden where she grew all our old favourites like leeks and Brussels sprouts. She'd been told they wouldn't grow in Nigeria. It did take a little ingenuity to make them grow well, but they invariably caused a sensation when they appeared fresh on her dinner table.

Behind the house was also a small swimming pool that always leaked. It was also next to impossible to keep clean as it had no built-in filtration system. It did, however, prove an excellent breeding pond for frogs and toads, and was a great place for the small crocodile I caught in the nearby river.

To one side of the main house was another small bungalow with a wriggly tin roof. This was the commandant's private guest house, in which official visitors were regularly accommodated. These included a number of senior officers visiting from the UK or from the headquarters further south, a few diplomats touring the region, occasional ministers from the federal government and the Commander in Chief of the newly independent Congolese army, General Josef Mobutu, and his wife Marie-Antoinette.

To the right of the house, shaded by a group of large mango trees, were three round huts with conical thatched roofs. These were stables. I never quite understood why it should be so, but in Zaria only the commandant was permitted to keep horses stabled in his garden. Some of the other officers, enthusiastic polo players among them, owned horses but had to stable their beasts in the horse lines, where a team of *doki* boys looked after them.

We kept no horses in the first year, but Dad and I used to go regularly and borrow mounts from the horse lines. We would then ride around the barracks, visiting the soldiers' quarters and less-visible parts of the establishment, stopping to watch the constant football games on the sports field. Besides giving us the opportunity to go riding together, it was an ideal way of ensuring all the soldiers saw their commanding officer regularly and being certain that he knew what was going on and was interested in them. Dad taught me that it was important to look after the men first as that built loyalty and excellence. Your own interests and needs are secondary.

The stables in the garden needed some repair before we could use them. It didn't happen until the following year. Then, after winning a goat-skinning competition at the Zaria Agricultural Show – which is a whole other story – I bought a horse from the Emir, so the stables had to be refurbished. Halissa was the first of several horses to occupy our stables. We had *doki* boy from the lines come to feed and attend to them, although whenever I was home, I looked after my own horse. This was partly because, having bought her, she was my responsibility, and also because the first *doki* boy beat her. He was sent back to the barracks with a flea in his ear and spent the next three months shovelling muck and polishing barracks floors.

Nigeria was a great country and, because it was new to me,

full of interesting things, people and places to explore. It didn't take long to acquire a coterie of local friends, both among the children of the European families stationed in Zaria and the local population. Even before I bought a horse, I began exploring the local bush, the markets and the old city.

Around the army camp, the countryside was intensively farmed, with fields of maize, millet and groundnuts covering most of the open spaces. To one side, beyond the cotton mill, was the Sabon Gari market which was the main commercial centre of Zaria. This comprised both a sprawling open-air market and the more formal section where banks, trading posts and offices were situated. It was a bustling place where you could find all manner of goods. Artisans plied their trades in small workshops, often consisting of no more than a workbench under a mango tree, and hawkers sold things as varied as traditional medical products – dried animal parts, special seeds, powders and potions and the like – or the advanced electrical appliances of the age.

On one occasion when I visited the Sabon Gari, there was a very eager crowd pressing around one particular trader in the section where most of the barbers usually operated. I'd been there a couple of weeks before to get my hair cut and now was curious to know what was causing so much excitement. Making my way forward in the crowd, I discovered one of the barbers was selling jars of Brylcreem. Nothing unusual in that, I thought, but then I discovered it wasn't being sold to dress anyone's hair.

Apparently a few weeks earlier a small shipment of this silky white hair cream had arrived and sold out within minutes of going on sale. A sharp-minded trader placed a bulk order for more and this too had sold out rapidly. Now a third, larger shipment had arrived and had just been unloaded from the train. The moment

At the Salah tribesmen dressed in their finest charged towards the Emir in salute.

anyone bought a pot, off came the lid, in went a finger and out came a large dollop that went straight into their mouth, to be savoured with obvious enthusiasm.

There was a logic of sorts. It's made of natural products, one of the main ones being coconut oil, which must have tasted good because Brylcreem had rapidly achieved almost magical status as food. As for making your hair shine, locally produced peanut oil did the same job and was reckoned to be far more economical.

Africa never failed to surprise.

HALF A MILE TO the south, across the shallow valley behind our house lay Brnin Zazau, the old city of Zaria. Surrounded by a high mud wall, the city had many ornate buildings, narrow alleys, small plazas and a broad open avenue leading up to the Emir's palace. This space was used once a year for the Salah, a traditional festival at which the Emir's subjects came in their tribal groups to declare their allegiance, pay their dues and submit their petitions.

It was a real spectacle. Dressed in their finest clothes, mostly mounted on horseback or camels, thousands of tribesmen in small groups charged up the avenue towards the Emir who was seated on a canopied dais. In colourful waves they advanced, reining in their mounts and stopping a few feet short of the podium. There, waving swords and lances and frequently firing ancient flintlock muskets, with clouds of dust stirred up by their animals' hooves swirling around them, each group delivered their salute.

Interspersed with the charging ranks of horsemen were groups of drummers and dancers and others who had come to pay their respects and join in the feasting and religious ceremonies that took place at the same time. Even witch doctors and sorcerers had their place, as every section of society was represented. Dad, as commander of the army base, sat with other local dignitaries and important visitors on a small dais to one side of the Emir's platform. The Salah lasted all that day and the next, with the feasting going on late into the night.

The Emir of Zaria was Alhaji Muhamadu Aminu, a large smiling man in his mid-fifties. He had been elected to his position some years before, having previously been the sheikh of the Sabon Gari. He was qualified for his position by being a member of one of the six families among which the emirate rotated. He had become *Sarkin Zazzau* when the previous holder of the office died.

Because of his work, Dad had frequent dealings with the Emir and we got to know him well. He even came to dinner in our house once, and on that occasion reduced his retinue to seven. It was a significant honour that he came at all, but coming with so few retainers was seen as a tremendous compliment, for he was

*Alhaji Muhamadu Aminu, Sarkin
Zazzau, the Emir of Zaria.*

normally attended by a crowd of at least forty. Except for his eldest son, we never met any of his family, although Mum was invited to visit his harem where she showed some of the women how
to knit. She was never sure of the exact status of any of the
women. Only one of them spoke any English and the knitting was
not a great success, although she did receive an elegant brocade
shawl as thanks for her efforts.

The Emir was passionately interested in horses and in horse
racing. This gave him an immediate affinity with Dad, who shared
his interest and used it to cultivate a fruitful relationship with the
palace. Both Dad and the Emir were on the committee of the local
jockey club and the Emir also supported the polo club, fielding a
team mounted on a fine string of ponies in every tournament.

The dye pits in Brnin Zazzau, where copious quantities of blue cloth were produced. Sheets of tie-died cloth can be seen hanging on the wall to dry.

The first time I met the Emir and shook hands with him, I got an interesting surprise. He had five fingers on his right hand. The extra digit was not merely a floppy appendage. It was a fully functional little finger, complete with bones, a finger nail, and a firm grip which made his handshake slightly disconcerting. I later discovered that his teenage son had the same anomaly.

In the back streets of the old city was the potters' quarter. There artisans transformed clay from the local river into a variety of interesting pots. These ranged from large cooking and brewing vessels to ornate pots and ewers coated in shiny gold mud, the latter being produced by just one family. The same gold mud was used to plaster most of the walls inside the Emir's palace, and also in the officers' mess at the army camp. It gave the rooms a warm glowing feeling, especially when illuminated by the reflected light of concealed copper wall sconces.

Not far from the pottery quarter were the dye pits. These were ten-foot deep wells with low rims, filled with indigo dye used to make various shades of the blue cloth for which the city was famous. The cloth was traded the length and breadth of West Africa. The most expensive – because it was steeped for longer and involved the most work – was an intense deep blue that almost glowed. It was burnished by being rubbed between two smooth stones with a smear of wax. The Tuareg people who lived in the desert to the north were particularly fond of it and the men wore large turbans made from ten-foot lengths.

There was always something to attract my interest and with my local friends I soon began exploring the countryside around Zaria and came to know it well. They were as enthusiastic as me in capturing and examining the small animals we encountered and one of them, Boniface, was particularly interested in small mammals. None of them, however, were keen to handle any of the snakes I picked up.

We soon knew the crossing points of the larger rivers, had visited most of the surrounding villages, and had walked miles down dried streambeds, gathering lumps of amethyst and other pretty stones which we traded in the market for snacks and other odd things. One of these bits of amethyst was only slightly smaller than a tennis ball, and looked like a fairy castle. I made a small wooden base for it to sit on and it served as a decoration in the family home for years. It still does.

The holidays were all too brief and before long it was time to return to the drudgery of school and the cold grey skies of England. I would gladly have stayed in Africa, but needs must and I had discovered one redeeming feature about our school: the river that ran through the school grounds. It presented interesting opportunities.

24 ~ Drama on the river

THE RIVER STOUR OFFERED a great escape route and I soon hatched a plan for using it. I needed a boat, so I made one in the carpentry shop. A kayak-style canoe was quick and easy to build, with thin stringers attached to light plywood frames and covered in canvas. I used a tin of motor grease to waterproof my first one, and in less than two weeks, it was ready to use. I launched it the first time in the mill stream because the water there was calmer than in the main channel or the weir pool. It worked well and I soon acquired some competence at handling it.

The Royal Marines base at Poole, only a few miles away, offered weekend training courses to youngsters interested in canoeing, so I applied to join one of these. Under their instruction, my interest flourished and I soon earned certificates of competence from the British Canoe Union. In the second year, I earned my instructor's qualification.

Canoeing became my escape whenever school became too restrictive and, to the frustration of those staff and senior boys who were trying hard to mould me like everyone else, I often absented myself down the river. Sometimes my absences lasted for several days. Since my parents were abroad, it would have been a bit difficult for the school to send me home for my misdemeanours, and they weren't about to give up the fees the Army paid for me to be there. Also, my brother had distinguished himself in a number of ways, and they probably hoped I might eventually follow his lead. The only time I did that was on the athletics field, and not because I was particularly athletic; I could simply jump higher than anyone else. Alistair had set a school record at six feet and half an inch. Two years later, I added an inch to that. I've been told that my record stood for five years, although now, like my other achievements, it's lost in the mists of history.

After I'd built a couple of canoes of different designs, others began to follow suit, but the sport was unregulated by the school and nobody else bothered to get any formal training. As a consequence of this, there were a number of silly incidents and near-accidents, mainly when the river was in spate, when currents could be unpredictable and hazards submerged beneath the roiling water. At such times, the weir pool became a churning mass of wild water with strong cross-currents and standing waves. It was a dramatic and exciting environment which, while being potentially very dangerous, provided the opportunity for some excellent white-water slalom canoeing.

I suggested to the school that it would be a good idea to have a proper canoe club and insist that anyone wanting to use the weir pool should pass basic safety and competence tests. Admittedly, part of my motivation for this was one of protecting what I had come to see as my own domain, and keeping idiots off the water, but I reasoned also that if someone inexperienced had an accident, it might put the weir pool off-limits to everybody. Since I was making headway in the season's national competitions, I didn't want my primary practice water to suddenly become inaccessible because someone else had messed up.

The school rejected my proposal, saying it wasn't necessary, and they didn't have a staff member with enough free capacity to take charge of a canoe club. I was bitterly disappointed but went off to a weekend competition and thought no more about it. I came back with a nice silver cup for the second year in a row.

On the following Monday, serendipity took a hand. It had rained hard throughout the weekend and the river level had risen dramatically. The Stour had overflowed its banks and now spread far across the water meadows on the opposite bank. So much water was coming over the sloping face of the main weir that a four-foot standing wave had formed across the bottom of it. Beneath that was a thirty-foot deep scour where the water had excavated a deep trench, so anything that became swamped there stood little chance of surfacing quickly and would almost certainly be dragged to the depths before being driven along the bottom to surface some distance downstream. Under flood conditions, that could be miles away.

On Sunday night, it had looked as if the river would overflow the near bank as well, so in the early morning one of the administrative staff decided to open the large sluice gate on the salmon run. This let a vicious cross-current into the weir pool, making the already turbulent water even more hazardous to anyone venturing out on it. By Monday morning, it was a churning brown maelstrom. The crashing roar of the water made normal conversation difficult for anyone standing on the bank of the weir pool.

At mid-morning break, I wandered down to look at the water, and consider whether it would be worth launching my canoe that afternoon. I found the headmaster standing by the rail, watching in horror as a boy in a red canoe floundered about in the middle of the rough water between the standing wave and the cross-current. He had none of the skill or the knowledge necessary to extract himself, was wearing neither a life jacket nor a safety helmet, and looked likely to capsize at any moment.

The headmaster, Ian Wallace, was aware of my training and that I had come back with a cup from the weekend's white-water competition. He asked what we could do to get the red canoe and its occupant out of his predicament.

"Not my problem," I replied. I felt slightly smug, despite the fact that Glyn Locke, the boy in trouble, was a friend of mine. "This was precisely why I said we needed a canoe club with regulations. You refused, so it's your problem."

"Could you get him out safely?"

"I could, but why should I? I didn't tell him to go in there. We need a club with proper regulations."

Seeing potential disaster staring him in the face, the headmaster was a pragmatist. "All right, you've got your canoe club. Now please go and rescue that idiot before he drowns."

That was enough for me. Shedding clothing as I headed for the hut where my canoe lived, a few yards away behind the bicycle shed, I hauled my boat from its rack, put on my lifejacket and helmet, and grabbed my paddle. Wearing nothing but my safety gear and a pair of underpants, I dumped the canoe on the bank at the edge of the weir pool, climbed in and fitted the spray deck. After a quick look to see where Glyn was, I leaned sideways, rolling over the edge into the water.

That form of launch leaves you upside down, so I first had to right myself. This was something I was trained for and had practiced many times, to the point that it had become almost automatic. I was also aware that, while technically it was the easiest and safest way to get into the water without help, it also looked spectacular and gave the headmaster a bit of a surprise that would reinforce my contention that, provided I got Glyn out safely, a properly regulated club with training was necessary.

But then Glyn was my pal and I wasn't going to let him drown.

It was harder than I expected to get across some of the strong currents and broken water to reach Glyn. Given how terrified he looked, I was amazed he was still afloat by the time I reached him. Like a rabbit dazzled by spotlights, he was transfixed by the maelstrom, unwilling – or unable – to move. He ignored the instructions I shouted at him, staring with a fixed gaze at the wave which held him in place while his canoe steadily filled with water.

So I had to come in diagonally and tip his canoe so that it capsized and he fell out over the bow of mine. I had lines strung from bow to stern on both sides of my canoe so he was able to grab one of these. He clung on for dear life while I heaved water aside and paddled hard to pull us backwards into the cross-current. When this caught my stern, it spun us around and out into the middle of the weir pool. From there it was a bit safer and largely a matter of hard paddling to bring us safely to the bank two hundred yards downstream.

The headmaster was clearly a quick thinker as he had sent someone for towels and blankets. As we emerged from the river, Glyn and I were swathed in warm, dry material, and willing hands helped pull my canoe from the water and carry it back to the shed.

During assembly the following Monday, the headmaster announced that henceforth canoeing would be restricted to members of the school canoe club, and only those who had attained a suitable qualified standard would be permitted in the weir pool. He appointed Tim Hooker as the staff member responsible for overseeing the club, and me as the club captain by virtue of my experience. Nothing was said about the incident at the weir pool although, of course, word had gone around and everyone knew what had happened.

We found Glyn's canoe a week later, after the flood had subsided. Its broken remains were wedged in some willow roots on the far bank, a hundred yards below where we came ashore and nine feet below the high water mark. Glyn never joined the canoe club, although others did, and it flourished while I was at the school.

The weir pool was only any use for slalom canoeing during the winter months, while the river was full. For the rest of the year, there were long clear reaches for both leisure and competitive paddling, above the weir where the rowing club operated. At first the rowers were resistant to canoeists getting in the way of racing fours and eights, but we reached an accommodation. Most of the canoeing activity took place during free time anyway, while rowing was confined to the couple of hours given over to sports every afternoon. Even so, a number of good long-distance and sprint paddlers were emerging by the time I left the school.

Canoeing didn't occupy all my time at school, but I have to admit it interested me far more than most of the lessons on offer. We commuted between classes and I'm sure my arms grew longer from carrying heavy loads of books. In those days, nobody had thought of using a backpack as students do today, and the old-fashioned school satchel was very infra dig, so you stacked your books and carried them under one arm.

The only lessons I really enjoyed were French, because I already had a good command of the language; geography, because it was about foreign places, many of which I had visited; and natural science, because it dealt with animals and plants which had been an interest since I first started exploring the bush in Northern Rhodesia. I found the other subjects stupefyingly boring, partly because of the way they were taught, but also because I found it difficult to see their relevance or understand why we had to study them. History was particularly tedious, and made more so by Mr Musson's insistence in droning on about why Napoleon invaded Russia and how he wanted to take over the whole of Europe.

One other source of relief I found was in the Combined Cadet Force. I'd grown up with the Army all around me, so the CCF was familiar territory. When I first got to Canford, every boy in the school had to be in the Corps, as it was known. Polishing boots and kit, rifle drill, and marching up and down were easy. Soon there were skills tests involving things like map-reading, navigation across country, and moving unseen as a tactical formation to surround a target in the wilds of Canford Heath. With my background of living in the bush, all this came naturally to me.

The heath was a wilderness of sandy heather, gorse and small boggy patches a mile to the south of the main school grounds. It stretched from there right down to Poole some miles away. The heath was in regular use for cross-country running, CCF exercises, several forms of nature studies, and a variety of illicit and less salubrious activities. It was an area I came to know intimately in my years at Canford.

I got on well with RSM Young, the only full-time staff member of the Corps, who looked after the armoury, the weapons and all the administration. I also got on well with Major Shorland-Ball, the house master of one of the boarding houses, who served as the commanding officer. Passing the various tests with ease, I got promoted, moving to the RAF section because they had a glider and went on visits to RAF stations where cadets were occasionally taken up in a plane. By the time I'd been in two and a half years, I found myself the senior NCO cadet, largely because the requirement to remain in the CCF until you left the school was rescinded. A lot of the senior boys gave up to concentrate on their academic studies and on social service activities. Their Wednesday afternoons now allowed them liberty to go into Wimborne, or to hide in the library while the rest of us put on our uniforms and played soldiers.

I was already interested in flying and, by transferring to the RAF section, I became eligible to apply for a flying scholarship. This was a scheme funded by the RAF to encourage youngsters to learn to fly by putting them through a qualifying course for their private pilot's licence. I had already passed a gliding course at Old Sarum on winch-launched Slingsby gliders. Now, understanding a bit more about how planes worked, I was keener than ever to learn to fly and the prospect of powered flying was an opportunity not to be missed.

My application was successful and in the summer of 1963 I did my training on Jackaroos and Tiger Moths at Thruxton, in Wiltshire. Both of these are biplanes, dating from the 1930s, the Jakaroo being a Tiger Moth that had been split down the middle and widened to accommodate four seats instead of just two. Over that a crude canopy, constructed like a greenhouse, was fitted. Both planes were powered by a single 120hp Gypsy Major engine and were fully aerobatic. However, we weren't allowed to do aerobatics in the Jackaroo because the plastic panes in the canopy had a propensity to fall out whenever the plane was inverted or subjected to negative G. The Jackaroo was originally made for the Australian market but a few remained in Britain where flying

My first solo flight was in this Thruxton Jakaroo.

clubs used them for *ab initio* training. We had nine of them at Thruxton, together with two Tiger Moths, one of which spent most of its time in pieces.

I made my first solo flight one evening after I'd made my fifth three-point landing in a row without bouncing. As we came to the end of our landing run, the instructor told me to taxi back to the take-off point for another circuit, but this time I would be doing it on my own. He climbed out to stand and watch, saying I should do a single circuit and then taxi back and pick him up when I landed.

The instructor climbing out of the plane must have been taken as a signal. The word spread on the flightline and as I began my take-off run, I looked across and saw all the other students and instructors standing in a line watching. I never expected to have an audience, although I soon discovered it was something that always happened when students made their first solo. I had five and a half hours dual time in my logbook and now I was going aloft on my own. This was freedom.

As the aircraft lifted into the early summer evening air, I

dreamed for a few moments about doing this over the African bush. That would be the ultimate freedom, and a few years later that dream came true. But on my first solo, it lasted a brief moment, and then my mind was back to concentrating on what I was doing, making a clean circuit and a smooth landing.

By the time I had picked up my instructor, the other students had begun putting the aircraft back in the hangar for the night, so we turned in that direction to deliver our plane as well. Mine was the last one in.

As I walked into the clubhouse, I dropped a sixpence in the slot machine and pressed the lever. The wheels spun and clunked to a stop in turn. Moments later the machine started clanking and a fountain of sixpences started spewing from the slot in the front. I quickly put my flying helmet underneath it to receive the £24 jackpot. If that wasn't an omen, I don't know what was. Whatever it was, it fuelled a damned good party that night, from which I was eventually poured into my bed.

I awoke early the following morning upside down at three thousand feet, in the back seat of the Tiger Moth, wearing only a pair of underpants, with my instructor's Labrador strapped in on top of me. Its tongue was flapping in the breeze, the drool from its mouth streamed back into my face. Waggling the stick let the instructor know I was awake, I could see him eyeing me in the small mirror attached to the tank above his head. He did another loop, a couple of slow rolls and a barrel roll, and then headed down to breakfast, disappointed that the aerobatics hadn't made me sick. I was quite relieved as I would have had to spend the rest of the day washing down the aircraft and I preferred to spend the time flying.

25 ~ Jungle drums

THE PARISH CHURCH AT Canford Magna lies within the school grounds. Although not unattractive, St Augustine's is a mishmash of a building, albeit a Grade 1 Listed building. Elements of it date back to the Saxon era; the Normans extended it and a number of neo-Gothic modifications have been added over the centuries. While still serving as the parish church, it came into regular use as the school chapel in about 1924, soon after the school was founded. It's still in regular use by the school, with the peal of six bells being rung every week.

It didn't take me long to realise that being a member of the campanology team gave me an easy excuse to avoid a number of activities and duties that bored me. Other than turning up to ring bells on Sunday mornings and for occasional weddings and other special events, the bell-ringers' duties and responsibilities were light. But the job provided opportunities to escape from the school routine by going off on excursions to ring bells in other churches around the region.

There were two regular parish ringers who joined us on Sunday mornings, Stan Chamberlain being the oldest and most consistent. By then in his seventies, he had been a Canford ringer since he was fifteen and only missed during the Second World War when he was overseas with the Army. He taught most of us all we knew about bell-ringing.

The bells were inspected regularly, with ropes and stops replaced when necessary. We had recently replaced most of the ropes, but for some reason the one supplied for the number five bell hadn't arrived with the rest, and only turned up a week later. Stan had supervised the changing of the ropes and when I offered to change No 5, as it was the bell I usually rang, he was happy enough to leave it to me.

So it was that on the evening of Friday 22 November 1963, I'd skived off prep and disappeared up the bell tower with another member of the team to change the rope on my bell. The other lad wasn't really needed, but took the excuse to come along because he was a radio buff and couldn't get very good reception on his short-wave set in the main school building. He had discovered, however, that by hanging a wire out one of the louvres on the church tower, he could pick up stations all round the world. So while I fiddled with the rope, he played with his radio.

That evening he chanced upon an American station and suddenly, through the crackling and fizz of the ether, we heard the dramatic announcement that President Kennedy had been fatally shot in Dallas. We looked at one another, not sure what we had heard, but a few seconds later the news was repeated.

While changing the other ropes the previous week, I had noticed a box of strange leather pads with straps attached and asked Stan what they were.

"Them's muffles," he told me. "We ha'nt used they since the King died." He went on to explain that the pads were strapped to the return stroke side of the clapper so that it rang true on the first stroke and muffled on the return. This half-muffled ringing was only used to mark momentous occasions like the death of a monarch or very important person.

When we heard the news about JFK, my friend and I looked at one another with the same idea.

"You go and call the team," I said, "and I'll start putting the muffles on the bells."

As he scampered down the ladder, I started strapping the leather pads onto the bell clappers. It was easier than it might have been because all the bells had been left standing, ready to start ringing in the morning without going through the discordant clanging caused by raising them from hanging rest to their inverted starting position. The clappers were all different sizes, but the muffles had a small brass disc engraved with its number on the strap.

Within ten minutes, the team assembled and I explained what we were going to do. We had a series of charts that listed the changes for different named peals, some of which could last for several hours. We chose a quarter peal that, according to the record book, had last been rung in Canford when King George V died, and hung that chart on the wall where we could all see it clearly as we stood in a ring by our ropes.

Fortunately a spare ringer had turned up so we elected him to call the changes. This made things simpler as everyone would know the next sequence as we reached the end of each round and the sequence could be maintained without interruption.

The sound of the muffled bells surprised all of us: it sounded as if the return was being rung far away. We soon got used to it and rang for ten minutes with only the caller's voice beside us and the bells above. Then the parish priest arrived. He was followed moments later by one of the school chaplains. Hot on their heels came the headmaster and one of the housemasters who lived on the campus, all wanting to know why we were ringing muffled.

"We're ringing for President Kennedy."

"And why would you ring for him?"

"Because he's been assassinated," I said.

"Has he? How do you know that?"

"It was on the radio."

They all looked confused until my friend explained about his short-wave radio and dangling the aerial from the bell tower to get better reception.

Moments later, Stan arrived and took over the tenor bell. The tenor moved up and took over No 5 and I took everyone else outside to explain without interrupting the changes. It was beginning to get crowded in the tower as other people arrived to find out why the bells sounded odd.

The following morning, I was called to my housemaster's study. I expected to be told off for another misdemeanour. This was getting to be a bit of a habit.

"Why did you instigate ringing a muffled peal last night?" he asked.

"It seemed the right thing to do," I replied. "President Kennedy had just been assassinated."

He looked puzzled. I continued: "He was a world leader and it seemed right to recognise that by ringing muffled."

"Yes, but why ring at all?"

"Jungle drums," I said.

"What the hell have jungle drums got to do with anything?"

"They're used to send messages, when news needs to be spread far and fast."

He looked puzzled again so I explained.

"We don't have drums here, and anyway nobody else would be able to understand them. But we do have bells, and they can be heard all down the river valley. People are used to hearing them, but not muffled. The different sound attracted attention. People came to find out what it was about. Nobody had heard the news before we started ringing. We spread the news."

"It certainly did that," he said. "All right, you can go." He waved me out of his study with the back of his hand.

Half an hour later, I was in the headmaster's office. This was getting monotonous.

"I seem to spend a lot of time crossing swords with you, young Mathie," he said as I entered. "But on this occasion you got something right. I have had phone calls from both the parish priest and Mr Chamberlain this morning, and the Dean from Wimborne Minster has just been on the phone complimenting the school's ringers on their tremendous effort last night and their inspired choice to ring muffled. I gather that was your idea."

"Yes, sir."

"So why did you do it?"

"Jungle drums, sir."

"Jungle drums? What do you mean? You were ringing bells."

"I think you'd better ask Mr Frewer, sir. He'll explain."

I left him looking puzzled.

26 ~ Strings and a strike

AT THE BEGINNING OF the autumn term, the Director of Music, a man popularly known as Crow Brown for reasons I never understood, came around and had us measure each other's left hands. Mine turned out to be by far the biggest in the school with a spread of over twelve inches from thumb to little finger, and my second finger was almost half an inch longer than anyone else's.

"That'll do," he declared. "You're it"

"I'm what?" I asked.

"You're now the double bass player in the school orchestra," he said, looking pleased.

"I don't play the double bass."

"That's all right, we'll teach you."

"But I don't even do music. I'm not sure the Army will pay for that as an extra, and I'm sure my Dad can't afford to."

He clearly wasn't going to take no for an answer. "Never mind that," he said. "We'll sort something out. Mrs Bridge will teach you. She'll see you in the music school after lunch."

As he left, I wondered if I should have said anything about Dad not being able to afford the lessons. Most of the boys here received no subsidy and came from prosperous, if not wealthy, families. They could be very cliquey and would now probably view me with more disdain than they already did because I had declared myself financially inferior. It wasn't something that had ever bothered me before, because the things I aspired to hadn't cost money or were within my own capacity to earn the where-withal by my own efforts. But I was aware that attitudes here could be selective, and I was already more than a slight misfit.

What the hell, I thought, I was being offered free music lessons. It would be churlish not to give it a try. So I went to see Mrs Bridge after lunch and began a whole new adventure. She was the wife of one of the chemistry masters and herself played double bass in the Bournemouth Symphony Orchestra. She was patient and unphased by my lack of musical knowledge. She maintained that since I could sing more or less in tune and had once tinkled out a few notes on the piano under the dreadful Miss Stein, I was capable of learning.

For three days each week, we met for half an hour after lunch and before the month was out, she had me scraping out recognisable notes. She also invited me to attend rehearsals with the BSO, where initially I just sat and listened. A few months later the principal conductor, Constantin Silvestri, invited all the members of the orchestra to bring their students to rehearsals as he was very keen to encourage young talent. He was very patient with us, meticulous in his dealings with the players, and he achieved a remarkable improvement in the orchestra's performing standard.

As a bonus, all of us who studied under members of the orchestra got free tickets to the concerts at the orchestra's home, the Bournemouth Winter Gardens. Maestro Silvestri even included us in one concert when the orchestra played Beethoven's

Sixth Symphony for a charity event. I was proud to have been a part of it.

Despite all this effort, I never actually played in a concert with the school orchestra. On the first two occasions when I should have played, I was away at a white-water canoeing event and was only saved from ignominy by coming back with a decent-sized silver pot on both occasions. On the third occasion, I had the runs, and couldn't sit still long enough to play because I was continually dashing off to the loo. By that time, two other boys had started learning the instrument, so the orchestra was not without a double bass.

When term resumed after Christmas in 1962, I was still struggling with lessons, and GCE exams were approaching. In February, history became the straw that broke the camel's back. Mr Musson was still droning on about Napoleon so I stopped going to his lessons and went to the library instead to try and make sense of the old maths exam papers I had obtained. Although I hadn't said anything to anyone else, I had more or less decided that I wanted to go into the RAF, and knew that I had to pass the exam to make this possible.

My absence wasn't reported until the third occasion, when the history master enquired if anyone knew where I was. Someone said that I'd said I had given up history. That's when the proverbial dung hit the ventilator. My housemaster summoned me and demanded that I explain myself. I told him I wasn't going to do history any more as I was learning nothing and needed to spend the time on more necessary subjects.

"You can't do that!" he exploded. "I won't allow it!" Neither pronouncement did anything to dent my resolve.

The cane was an instrument of punishment still in common

use, both by masters and senior prefects in those days. Now Mike Frewer seized his cane and threatened me with it, commanding me to bend over so he could thrash me.

He was more than startled when I grabbed it out of his hand, snapped it in two and threw it back at him, turning to leave his study and being careful not to slam the door.

I retired to my room after the confrontation with my house-master. We had moved, as the years passed, from a large junior common room and open dormitories, to smaller common rooms and eventually to individual study bedrooms. By the time this incident happened, I inhabited a small room up in the attic, with a window looking out on a wide lead-lined gutter. This lay below the huge stained glass window which adorned the western end of the great dining hall.

Half an hour later, there was a polite tap on the door and my house tutor, Robin Whicker, came in. He was young, very bright, relatively new to the school, still unmarried and lived in a small flat in the building. Plonking himself on my bed, he said quietly, "I think we need to have a chat."

We talked for two hours and missed supper, but at least it was constructive. By the end, he understood what I was trying to do and, while not approving of my method, was at least willing to try and accommodate my need. All the same, he felt that going on strike and the business of the cane would probably earn me an uncomfortable interview with the headmaster. If I survived that without being thrown out, he would try and help me, but I might have to make a few compromises.

After that he told me to put my jacket on and come with him as we both needed food. He piled me into his Mini, drove to Wimborne and bought me fish and chips. When I said I felt I ought to pay for it, he insisted, saying it might be my last meal as the condemned man because the headmaster would undoubtedly want to see me tomorrow.

Robin Whicker had a wonderful sense of irony.

27 ~ The General's interpreter

MY INTERVIEW WITH IAN Wallace, the headmaster, did not go
well. To say he was furious at my temerity would be a gross
understatement. Had I been a British-based pupil, he would probably have sent me home on the spot, my minor achievements that
brought honour to the school notwithstanding. As it was, it would
take a bit of arranging because my parents were in Nigeria and
communications were not as instant as they are today. Even so, an
early break was inevitable.

I had by this time set up the canoe club, which was running
smoothly and was well-supported. I had also contributed five
silver cups for canoeing to the school's trophy shelf. They would
all have to go back next year, unless I won them again, which
wasn't likely, but for the time being they looked good in a line. I
had also achieved my gliding certificate, had won a place on the
course to get my private pilot's licence, was the senior cadet in the
CCF, and had won a local cross-country race.

It is doubtful whether these achievements contributed anything to Mr Wallace's decision since they were individually relatively minor but, worse still, none of them were academic. He was

very much an academic headmaster, and pushed hard to raise the school's standards. In this I was probably a disappointment to him. Nonetheless, he wasn't going to abandon me completely.

He decided that I should retire early for the Easter holidays and review my situation and actions at home. By the time I returned for the summer term, he expected a very different and more cooperative attitude. A telegram had been sent to my father and a flight had been arranged for the following evening. My house tutor would take me to the airport and see me onto the plane.

Walking down the aircraft steps and across the apron to the arrivals hall at Kano airport in the early morning felt like walking out of the prison gate. The sun was just beginning to warm the air, the smells of Africa mingled with those of burned aviation fuel to produce a heady mixture, and the sea of smiling black faces along the balcony waiting to welcome their loved ones home lifted my spirits. I hadn't been looking forward to the rocket I knew I was about to get from my father, even though I knew I deserved it. In the end he said very little, simply asking for my side of the story and warning me that Mum was most upset. I should think about what I was going to say to her on the way down to Zaria.

Mum was not at the house when we reached home; she was down in the barracks running a baby clinic for the soldiers' wives. Dumping my suitcase in my room, I went out to the stable, slipped a bridle over Halissa's ears and, not bothering with a saddle, swung myself up onto her back. We cantered all the way to the clinic where I tied her reins to a mango tree outside. As I walked in, Mum was explaining to one of the women why she should feed her baby well. She turned and gave me a quick but fierce hug and then turned back to the woman.

"This is my baby," she announced. "If you want your son to

grow up big and strong like him, you must feed him as I have shown you. Then when he is this big, you can beat him, because he will need it." With that she turned and gave me the most almighty whack round the ear. I knew what it was for, and it told me exactly how upset she was. She didn't have to say anything.

My ear stung for days.

When he came home from his office in the evening, Dad announced that next week we would have a visitor. The commanding general of the newly independent Congolese army was coming for an official visit to learn how the Nigerian soldiers were trained. He would be bringing his wife with him and they were to stay in our guest bungalow but eat with us. The general was bringing an interpreter with him for his official duties but, since his wife spoke no English, I would have to help my mother entertain her by being their interpreter when the general was working.

When Dad brought the general home for lunch on the first day, he informed me there had been a slight change of plan. The interpreter who accompanied the party had been provided by the Nigerian government. He came from Cameroon, where they spoke both French and English. This morning had demonstrated that his command of both languages was deficient, and he didn't understand any of the military terminology. The general was not pleased, as he had come to learn and needed good translation.

"You've grown up with the Army all your life," Dad said, "and you speak French. Now you can redeem yourself for the fiasco at school by being the interpreter for this visit."

One of the young Nigerian officers was married to a girl from Niger who spoke both French and English, so she was drafted in to replace me and translate for the ladies. This proved to be an inspired choice since the general's wife wanted to have her hair done in a Nigerian corn-row style and Nasima knew exactly where to take her. She and Mum were friends anyway, so it was easily organised.

After lunch, I accompanied Dad and General Josef Mobutu back to the barracks to continue the official part of his visit. He proved to be a charming man, well-versed in military organisation and very interested in Dad's training methods. He asked lots of questions, was patient while I translated the answers and often came back with secondary questions or points of discussion. Although he spoke Belgian French, he was easy to understand and we had no problem in communicating clearly. By the time the afternoon was almost over, I had got my brain in gear and was providing almost simultaneous translation, which greatly accelerated the discussions. That evening the general was the guest of honour at a formal dinner in the Officers' Mess. I, of course, had to attend as interpreter, remaining just behind his left shoulder throughout the evening. A hasty meal had been provided for me beforehand, while the general was getting dressed, since I would have to translate continuously throughout the reception beforehand, as well as during the meal and the speeches that followed it.

By the time I retired to my bed that night, I was beginning to wonder if going on strike over history lessons had been quite such a clever move. Still, it had been an exciting and interesting day.

The second day of General Mobutu's visit was an activity day which began with shooting on the range. He was keenly interested to see the level of discipline and skill the Nigerian soldiers displayed. He seemed impressed by their weapons discipline and insisted that his Aide de Camp get details of the full weapons training and shooting programme.

Having watched the range drills for an hour, our attention was turned to a fire and movement exercise in the nearby bush. With the soldiers moving towards a designated target, we took ourselves to a small hill that overlooked the training area to watch. As we walked up the hill, I spied something familiar and interesting in a bush and stepped aside for a moment to investigate. I returned a few moments later with a beautiful bright green snake in my hand. The ADC leapt back in alarm when he saw this, insisting it was dangerous. General Mobutu merely smiled and asked me if it had rough or smooth scales.

"Rough scales, sir," I replied.

"Then it is not poisonous," he said. "It is probably an emerald tree snake. We have these snakes in Lisala, where I grew up. They are very pretty and eat frogs and weaver birds."

I was amazed at the scope of this man's interests.

That afternoon we trooped over to Brnin Zazzau to pay a courtesy visit to the Emir. Dad had telephoned to inform the Emir's secretary that he had an important visitor. To foster good relations, he thought a brief visit might be of interest to both. The Emir had a number of people in his court who hailed from northern territories close to Niger and who spoke French and Hausa, so I was freed for an hour to accompany the ladies to the inner parts of the old city. Mum was keen to show Mme Mobutu the dye pits and the exotic cloths they produced. There were also other market areas in the old city which, besides being distinctly Nigerian in character, were also unique to Zaria.

That evening, the general and his wife came to our house to have dinner. The Nigerian District Commissioner, Ali Akilu, also spoke quite good French. He joined us, along with Bill Dexter and his wife. Bill was the general manager of the United Africa Company and one of the most prominent businessmen in the area.

The general and his wife were excellent company and seemed to enjoy their meal. He expressed himself surprised and most impressed when he asked to meet the cook to compliment him on the food and I explained that it was my mother who had done all the cooking because the meal had to be special. He exchanged a few words with his wife in their own language and Mum noted a significant look he gave her. I wondered if Mme Mobutu ever cooked for his guests.

After the meal, sensing that Mme Mobutu needed the bathroom Mum nipped in first to check that the place was clean and presentable. She returned a moment later asking that I go and remove the snake which had coiled itself round the toilet pedestal before our guest went in there. I took one of Dad's walking sticks and went to investigate.

The snake had moved and was now coiled up on top of the seat. Inevitably it was a cobra and it raised its hood as I opened the bathroom door. A quick whack with the stick and I was able to pin its head down with the handle long enough to get a safe grasp on it. As I lifted it up, it coiled and writhed, wrapping itself round my arm. There was no way out to the garden without passing through the room where everyone was now seated for after-dinner coffee and it was noticeable that only my parents, who were used to me catching snakes, and General Mobutu, showed no fear.

After I had taken the snake out, Mme Mobutu insisted my mother should accompany her to the bathroom in case any other animal was there.

The following morning, the Army held a formal parade at which General Mobutu took the salute. Having worn khaki all week, Dad put on his own regimental uniform with tartan trews

General Mobutu with my Dad, touring the military establishment in Zaria.

to honour the occasion. After lunch in the Mess, we all trooped out to Zaria's small airport where the general's plane was waiting to take him home.

The general's wife, Marie Antoinette, and his mistress, Bobi Ladawa, had already boarded the plane. For the formal departure, four of us walked across the scorching concrete and stopped at the foot of the boarding steps. The general turned to Commissioner Ali Akilu, dressed in brilliant white robes and a colourful embroidered hat, offering his hand to say his goodbyes.

The general turned to my Dad, still resplendent in highland regimental uniform. Shaking hands, the general offered his profuse thanks for the hospitality he and his entourage had received in our home, and also for the invaluable insights that his tour of the country's primary military training station had given him. Dad spoke just enough French to understand and to offer his own farewell and good wishes for a safe flight, so I remained silent.

With the formalities concluded, the two soldiers faced one another again and exchanged smart salutes before General Mobutu turned to climb the steps. As he put his foot on the first step, he paused, turned back and addressed me.

"Thank you for your service. It has been very helpful to my mission here. How much have they paid you for your work?"

"Thirty pounds, sir."

"You are worth much more than that," he said. Reaching into his breast pocket, he withdrew a bundle of notes which he thrust into my hand. "This is my thanks for your service," he said, "And I give you my personal invitation that if you ever come to my country, you must come and visit me in my home."

"Thank you sir, I shall remember that."

"I shall expect you," he said, shaking my hand and meeting my eye with a look that made me wonder if he knew something I didn't about the future. Turning again, he climbed the steps to stand beside his wife at the aircraft's door. They paused for a moment, waving to the small party on the apron, before disappearing inside.

The aircraft's door closed, the propellers moved spasmodically and the four engines coughed in turn, belched smoke, and growled into life before settling down to a throaty rumble. Minutes later, the shiny military transport moved off along the taxiway to the end of the runway. As the engines roared and the plane began to roll, a man seated on a camel, outside the airport's small terminal building, raised a huge traditional trumpet to his lips and blew a long, drawn-out note that echoed mournfully over the sweltering airfield until the roar of the departing plane drowned it.

As we walked back to the car, Dad said: "That seemed to go well. Thank you." He never made any other reference to the reason why I'd been there at that time, so I guess I must have redeemed myself.

Ten years later, I found myself in Kinshasa, the capital of Zaïre, where Mobutu was president. In the intervening years, the Congo had endured two revolutions and a savage civil war, after which Mobutu had seized power. In pursuit of an idealised concept of African authenticity, he changed the country's name to Zaïre, and his own name to a stylised African one. He was now called Mobutu Sese Seko Kuku Ngbendo Wa Za Banga. This was a grandiose title stating that he was an indefatigable warrior who, through his own endurance and fortitude, conquered all obstruction and left burning ruins in his wake. It was an image that fitted ill with the slightly shy, highly intelligent and quick-learning man I had met in Nigeria.

I did indeed go to the palace to see him*, but that was still a long way in the future.

* see *Supper with the President*, 2011

28 ~ Crocodiles and bush trips

WHEN I WASN'T OUT wandering around the bush with my
Nigerian friends, I spent many afternoons in Zaria beside the
camp swimming pool. Its original purpose had been for teaching
the soldiers to swim, but that use had declined under the previous
commander of the depot. By the time we came, it had become
more a club for the officers and their families and only the boys
from the army school got occasional swimming lessons. Dad set
about changing that and reintroduced swimming for all troops
during morning sessions.

Small membership fees paid by the officers' families enabled
the club to open to civilian families in the area in the afternoons,
and kept the whole thing financially viable by paying for its cleaning and filtration plant. Sometimes, particularly at weekends, the
pool could get very crowded.

Tommy Storey was a friend of ours who ran the cotton mill
on the edge of the Sabon Gari market. Cotton was extensively
grown all over the northern region. Farmers brought their raw
cotton to the mill where the husks and seeds were removed and it
was washed. The clean cotton was then carded to straighten out

the fibres and packed in bales for shipment to the last remaining spinning mills that were still operating in Lancashire. Tommy was interested in wildlife, his house being a sanctuary for all sorts of animals. He had a number of resident monkeys and bush babies, which had more or less free range about the place, a selection of parrots and other exotic birds that lived in huge cages under the flame tree at the back of the house, and a tame warthog that lived in his garden. He also had two young crocodiles, about three feet long, which inhabited his garden pond, together with a selection of snakes and scorpions in glass tanks under a thatched awning.

After many of my trips onto the hinterland, my first port of call on the way home was to Tommy's house to bring him any interesting creatures I had brought back, or to discuss ones I had seen and not recognised. He held a fund of useful knowledge, which he was always ready to share. He also had an indefatigable sense of fun, which occasionally got him into trouble.

This happened once at a formal dinner party to celebrate the Queen's birthday. Guests wore evening dress, the table was laid with crystal glasses and the silverware was brightly polished. The woman sitting across the table from Tommy suddenly shrieked "He's got a snake!" just as a small serpent that Tommy had caught on his way to the party and tucked into the inside pocket of his dinner jacket, poked its head out of his collar. Disturbed by the noise, the snake withdrew its head and headed down his sleeve instead. Those seated either side of the woman reassured her that she was seeing things, that it had been just a trick of the light. A few minutes later, when she had been calmed, the serpent emerged from Tommy's left cuff and headed directly across the table in her direction.

Glass, china and cutlery went flying as the screaming woman

fled from the table. The falling tableware frightened the snake, which turned back and disappeared into the inviting darkness of Tommy's right cuff as he reached across the table to retrieve it

"Really Tommy! How could you?" commented the hostess in mild reproof, automatically assuming that he must have been responsible for the woman's outburst.

Tommy raised both his hands defensively, palms outwards to show that he was holding nothing and muttered, "Nothing to do with me. I fear the wine must have disagreed with her if she's started seeing things."

Of course everyone present knew Tommy and suspected he did have a snake with him, even if only one or two of us had actually seen it. But by then we were all accustomed to his foibles, and few of us took much notice of them.

A few weeks later, Tommy decided to join us at the swimming pool one Saturday afternoon. When he arrived, the pool was so crowded it was difficult to get in, and even the changing room was blocked with a queue of people. Tommy went home and returned half an hour later, already changed with his swimming trunks under his street clothes. He walked in through the gate, threw his two baby crocodiles into the water and began to take off his street clothes beside the pool. By the time he was undressed, the pool was empty except for the two crocodiles swimming lazy lengths. Tommy dived in to join them and apart for a couple of us, nobody was willing to go in the pool until he'd climbed out and removed his pets.

I LEARNED A LOT about the people of the region from a CMS missionary, Peter Lapage, who had become a friend of the family. He piqued my interest and, together with my friends Boniface and

Tuesday, both of whom were mission-educated boys, I spent quite
a lot of time out in nearby villages. Sometimes, when neither of
them was free, because they both worked, I took Halissa and went
exploring on my own.

A horse proved to be a good introductory mechanism because
the Hausas are an equestrian people at heart. For generations,
they provided cavalry for their rulers and were fundamental to the
glory of the Hausa Empire which once covered the whole of
northern Nigeria and parts of Niger and Chad.

Anyone riding a good horse was likely to arouse interest.
Halissa was a very good horse, having come from the stables of
the Emir. She was not unknown among the tribes. Others had
tried to buy this horse, believing she would make a good polo
pony. Some had offered large sums, but all had been refused. For
reasons of his own, the Emir chose to sell her to me for a ridiculously low price, which caused endless speculation and more than
a little envy in some quarters.

Now Halissa acted like a badge of favour, and ensured that I
was courteously received wherever I went on her.

I had another reason for going out to one particular village.
My friends and I had reached that age when girls were never far
from our thinking.

My friend Tuesday Molosi was the youngest of six brothers
whom his father, a bible-reading Christian, had named Matthew,
Mark, Luke, John and Daniel. He desperately wanted a daughter
and, on finding he had yet another son, he left his wife to name
the child. She couldn't think of an appropriate biblical name, so
she named him Tuesday, because that was the day of the week
when he was born.

His father took little interest in his youngest son, his sole contribution being to ensure he got a place at the mission school when he was old enough.

Growing up in a predominantly male household, with four of his brothers already married, it was hardly surprising that Tuesday became very interested when he discovered that Boniface had three sisters. His interest soared when he discovered they were all very pretty, our age, and unmarried.

Boniface's home village, about twenty-five miles from Zaria, became one of our more frequent destinations when the three of us went rambling in the bush. Normally we would begin in the Sabon Gari and catch a mammy wagon ride for the first part of the trip. Mammy wagons are usually owned by women and are the workhorses of West Africa. They carry everything, including passengers perched atop their primary cargo. Most have regular routes, although these can change without notice at the whim of the owner or an influential passenger.

The day we made our first visit to Boniface's village, our mammy wagon dropped us off early because the owner's sister was on board and wanted to divert to visit a friend. As a result, we had to walk across country and camp out in the bush overnight. Neither of the others was experienced at living rough in the bush, so the skills I had learned in East Africa came in useful. Even so, they didn't stop us having a surprise visitor during the night. It was an experience that still makes the hairs on the back of my neck tingle. The memory of the leopard which licked my toes during the night is something I shall never forget*.

Boniface's sisters proved to be every bit as beguiling as we'd hoped, and they were delightful company. That expedition was

* see *Man of Passage*, 2006

but the first of many. It was, however, marred by the shocking news we received on our return to the Sabon Gari. An hour and a half after it dropped us off, the mammy wagon on which we had begun our trip had been involved in a crash. Several passengers were killed and the wagon was a write-off. The name board above that mammy wagon's cab had proclaimed it to be 'No Hurry to Die'.

29 ~ Car repairs and games with pagans

TWO WEEKS BEFORE I was due to return to school in England, we made a long trip to the northernmost reaches of the country. Dad and his officers mounted regular recruiting expeditions and this was one of those. The area selected was Bornu, up in the far northeast, near Lake Chad and the northern Cameroon border. This is the area now largely controlled, or at least terrorised, by Boko Haram terrorists. Back in the 1960s, the army draft intake had included recruits from this region and without exception they had outperformed all the others in their intake. So Dad had decided to try and recruit more men from the region.

The further north we went, the worse the roads became. None had ever had tarmac surfaces and few had seen a road grader since they had been churned up by mammy wagons during the last rains, three months before. It was slow going, which gave us plenty of time to study the countryside. We were travelling in Dad's staff car, with his regular driver Corporal Audu Katsina at the wheel. Ten miles outside Gwoza, the head gasket blew. Fortunately there was a convoy of military vehicles coming up some miles behind, ready to transport any recruits back to the Depot in Zaria.

Mum and Dad transferred themselves to one of the Land Rovers when the convoy caught up, while Alistair and I elected to remain with Cpl Audu and help him repair the car. I wasn't sure how much help I could be, but the opportunity to wander around a new and unfamiliar part of the bush appealed and I had seen a small settlement less than a mile back. Alistair loved fiddling with anything mechanical and was keen to get his hands into the engine alongside Cpl Audu. So we stayed.

Before I could set off to explore the village, a line of five near-naked women approached us. They wore nothing but smiles and bunches of fresh leaves tied front and back to the string of beads that circled their waists. Their hair was woven into complicated braids, adorned with cowrie shells and silver coins. In addition, their skins were covered with keloid scars which formed thousands of closely spaced small lumps in intricate swirls, stripes and spirals over most their upper bodies. They approached with their hands out, hoping for some cash, but were disappointed because we had no coins to give them.

Hoping he might know, because he came from Katsina, the neighbouring state in the northern region, I asked Audu if he knew which tribe the women were from.

He stared at them for a long moment and said in a tone I had never heard him use before, "Those are not women, they are savages! These creatures are pagans. Have nothing to do with them." He stared for a bit longer before he turned away in disgust and, spanner in hand, buried his head in the engine compartment to continue dismantling.

Apart from cleaning pieces of engine in a tin of petrol and lay-

ing them out on sheets of newspaper as Audu and Alistair disman-
tled the engine, there was little I could contribute. Since they needed me to do this job, I had no opportunity to wander off and
explore the huts I had seen.

Under the blazing sun, the afternoon wore on, and I thought
about what Audu had said. Prejudice, it seemed, could be found
in any society; it wasn't just ours. All the same, the women had
been an interesting group, the eldest being a woman of about
forty, who I could see showed signs of aging. The youngest was a
girl of my own age, whose attractions had been most evidently on
display and who knew how to ensure they were noticed. Their
skins were all significantly blacker than most of the people we had
seen before, and they positively glowed in the sunlight because
they had rubbed their bodies with oil. I wished I'd had a camera
so I could show Tuesday and Boniface when we got back to Zaria,
and then I wondered how they, as good Christian boys, would
react. Audu was nominally a Muslim, and I knew that meant he
was not supposed to look at naked women. All the same, he'd
looked at these five, carefully, before turning away.

The sun was almost at the horizon by the time Audu and
Alistair had replaced the burst gasket and reassembled the engine.
It started first time when Audu pressed the button and ran
smoothly. Even so, he said we would need to go slowly for fifteen
minutes and then stop and tighten some nuts, as he hadn't had a
torque wrench, whatever that was, and he needed to make sure
the cylinder head was properly settled before he drove it hard. He
was a good mechanic as well as a good driver.

While the women had wandered off once they realised there
were not going to be any hand-outs, our presence by the roadside
soon attracted a crowd of small children. They appear out of

nowhere wherever you stop in Africa, to stand and stare at any unfamiliar sight. Cars were uncommon enough, but even fewer white people came to this part of the country, so we were naturally a source of interest. Like the women, the children were naked. Only the older ones, presumably those who had reached puberty, were wearing bunches of leaves like the women. This lot were less restrained than the women and all wanted to shake my hand, run their fingers over my pale skin, and feel my hair. I took my shirt off to show them that apart from the colour of my skin I was no different from them and felt numerous curious fingers stroking my back.

As he lifted out another piece of engine, Audu told me I should keep away from the boys. They were unnatural. I asked him how they were unnatural. Did they eat people?

"They are savages and pagans. They have no god in them," was all he would say, his tone as derisive as it had been about the women. All I saw was a crowd of children, curious about strangers who had stopped on the road near their home.

There was a bag of old tennis balls among our luggage, so I searched in the boot and brought one out. I bounced it on the ground a few times, then tossed it into the crowd of children, causing shrieks of delight and an immediate stampede. As the road was the clearest open space, most of the game that followed took place on it, but occasionally wandered off the sides as children crashed about among the roadside bushes. Even then, the enthusiasm of pursuit was undiminished and the squeals of happy delight were continuous. Several times the ball came flying back in my direction and I kicked it back into the crowd. Although many of the children were scrawny, they seemed to have limitless energy and were remarkably agile and quick on the turn.

When Audu started the engine, the game petered out. As we

were piling the tools back into the car, a boy came forward and offered me the ball. I shook my head, indicating that he should keep it, but he didn't seem to understand. I took it from him and threw it into the back of the crowd, holding up my hands to indicate that it was not to come back. The laughter and shouts of delight resumed with the chase that this precipitated and, as we climbed into the car to drive on, their game drifted back down the road, towards the settlement.

30 ~ Compromise with strings

MY RETURN TO SCHOOL was undramatic and nobody seemed to have noticed my early absence at the end of the previous term. A few of my classmates asked if I'd had a good time in Africa, more from politeness than any real interest. Alistair was now busy with his nose in his books, getting ready for his A Levels, so I saw very little of him. He had not come to Nigeria this time, preferring to go off on a cycling tour of Norway with friends. He'd had long discussions with Dad during the previous holiday because he'd decided he was going to join the RAF. Like me, he wanted to fly, had applied to Cranwell and had been offered a place dependant on his obtaining good exam results. Dad had not been pleased. He'd hoped his sons would follow him into the Army, to his own regiment. All but two sons of the family had served in it since it was raised in 1777. The two who didn't go into the regiment went to the *kirk*, which was acceptable in our part of Scotland where tradition was still strong, if often unseen.

Dad did everything he could to persuade Alistair that the Army would be a better career, but my brother was adamant. All that furore made me think twice about saying too much about what I wanted to do when I left school, and after my recent misdemeanour I didn't feel like becoming the target of any heavy-handed persuasion. Anyway, the regiment had changed. The Highland Light Infantry had been amalgamated with the Royal Scots Fusiliers in 1959 to become the Royal Highland Fusiliers, which had changed its character considerably. While the regiment went on to distinguish itself in Aden, Northern Ireland and other theatres of operation, it wasn't something I yearned to be part of. Ironically, today as I write this, a battalion of the RHF is one of the few remaining elements of the great Scottish regiments still serving in the British Army. Almost all the others have been disbanded.

I was invited to an early interview with the house tutor who had been busy in my absence. He had spoken to the history master and agreed that I should attend his lessons, sit at the back, but take no part in the class. I could spend those periods working my way through maths exam questions, which would be set for me by one of the teachers in that department. Although we talked about it, there wasn't really any room for discussion and I soon realised I'd got off lightly. I thanked him for the efforts he had made on my behalf and rose to leave. That was when he demanded his pound of flesh.

"There's one small thing you could do in return," he said.

I sat down again and listened.

The school had been given a harpsichord – in kit form. It needed somebody to assemble the kit. Since I had built no fewer than eight kayaks and canoes of different designs in the woodwork shop, and I had made a copy of a Jacobean table with barley sugar twisted legs, Freddy Bagshaw, the woodwork teacher had noted that I had a little skill in working with wood. He wondered if I might be persuaded to take on this task. Robin felt this gesture of service to the school might offer a suitable recompense for my misdemeanour, and would give me something I was good at to exercise my spare energy on.

It was presented as a compromise I could not gracefully refuse.

I'd never seen a harpsichord, and hadn't a clue how one worked. From the description, it sounded fiendishly complicated and I hoped there were some good instructions in the kit. When it came to the musical part of it, I didn't have a clue. The little I'd learned about music from my efforts with the double bass was hardly a qualification for something like this. That instrument only had four strings, unlike this which had about eighty. Not to worry, another boy, an organ scholar no less, had volunteered to do the strings and tuning when it came to that part. My job was to assemble the body of the thing, to make the keyboard and to construct all the fiddly little jacks that plucked the strings.

I felt cornered, but also challenged. Stalling for time, I asked if I could have a look at the project before deciding.

One look at the disorganised heap of timber and assorted bits of metal told me that several other people had already looked at the project and given up. The instruction sheet had been mislaid and Freddy Bagshaw was in despair. Unfortunately the box had been opened in his absence and, since the thing had been a gift to the music department, all the pieces had been brought down to the woodwork shack from there. Freddy wasn't even sure if everything was in the pile. Going to the music school to enquire, I found only Mrs Bridge, waiting to give me a double bass lesson. She knew nothing about it but suggested the best thing would be to look at an original instrument and see if it was possible to identify the different components. She would take me at the weekend to look at one in a large country house. Meanwhile we had strings to scrape and I hadn't touched an instrument for six weeks.

We had an interesting outing that Sunday afternoon deep into the wilds of Somerset to visit an old manor house where there was a fine old harpsichord in regular use. The owner was more than willing to lift the lid and explain its workings and construction to me. She even offered to come over and look at our instrument as it took shape, if that would be of any assistance. It most definitely would, I assured her.

As we went down the front steps to take our leave, Mrs Bridge stumbled and fell, badly twisting her ankle. She insisted it was not broken, but she couldn't put any weight on it. Neither could she drive. There was nothing else for it: I picked her up, put her in the passenger seat and got behind the wheel myself.

"But can you drive?" she asked, sounding doubtful.

"Yes. Corporal Audu taught me in Nigeria. I drove every day out there." This was entirely true and, although I had not been allowed to drive on the open road, I had been permitted to drive anywhere within the military encampment. Cpl Audu had taught me on our old Vanguard estate, but during this last visit Mum had exchanged it for a Morris Traveller. Mrs Bridge had a Mini Traveller, which was very similar to drive.

As we set off I could see her ankle swelling, so I drove straight to the nearest hospital with an accident department. They X-rayed it, decided it was broken, and three hours later we left there with her on crutches, her left foot firmly encased in a large white plaster cast. I dropped her off at her home and her husband drove me back to school, whining and wittering that it wouldn't have happened if I hadn't asked her to take me to see some twangy piano thing. I didn't bother telling him it was her idea, not mine.

I didn't feel in the least bit guilty or under any obligation but I did agree, on the basis of that outing, to try and build the harpsichord.

Two weeks later, the plan for the kit turned up. We never found out where it had been, but one evening I went down to the workshop and found it lying on top of the frame I had assembled the previous evening.

It took most of the summer term to build the instrument. The actual woodwork wasn't too complicated. The time-consuming bit, most of which I did in my own study, was making the fiddly little jacks which plucked the strings. These consisted of thin slices of wood about six inches long and three-quarters of an inch wide, with a small hinged insert in a slot near one end. This had a fine hair spring pressing on the back of it and a small peg, made of hardened boiled leather, sticking out like a beak from its front face. Pressing a key on the keyboard lifted the jack so that the beak came in contact with a string, effectively plucking it. It was shaped so that it would slide past the string when the key was released and the jack descended. When the harpsichord evolved into the pianoforte, small hammers that were designed to strike the strings, and therefore produce a greater range of sound, replaced the jacks.

Eventually I finished the instrument and it was played for the first time when the school choir joined forces with their counterparts from a girls' school for a performance of Handel's *Messiah* in a Bournemouth church.

31 ~ Off to sea

THE SUMMER TERM GROUND on. The prospect of the free-dom of the African bush was the only light at the end of a dark and generally tedious tunnel. May was exam time and, for me, the dreaded GCE O Levels. The first was a French aural test. The examiner asked about my interests and I talked enthusiastically for half an hour about canoeing and flying. It was evident quite early on that he understood very little of what I talked about as he knew nothing about either subject or its terminology. But he seemed pleased as we parted, saying he'd enjoyed our talk. This put me in a good mood as I approached the rest of the exams.

History was the first written paper. Although I'd been allowed to stop studying history, part of the deal had been that I would attempt the exam. To my great amusement, there was not a single question about Napoleon, the original source of my boredom. I was amazed a few months later to discover that I'd passed with a respectable grade.

Mathematics, the subject I dreaded, was the last exam and I approached it fatalistically, thinking that if the questions didn't make sense I would simply walk out. Luck must have been with me for I understood just enough questions to do the required number. Even so, I still ground to a halt half an hour before the end of the set time. I sat for a few minutes, twiddling my thumbs and wondering what to do. The invigilator cast a few speculative looks in my direction. Eventually he started walking toward me. I didn't feel like an interrogation about why I'd stopped, so I got up and left the examination hall before he reached me.

Realising there was likely to be an inquest, and taking advantage of the rest of the school being busy with lessons and exams, I went back to my study, changed into sports kit, collected a few useful items and headed for the canoe shed.

I had recently built a long, slim sea kayak, which travelled swiftly down the lower reaches of the River Stour. Nobody saw me leave and within twenty minutes I was hauling it out of the water to portage round a weir with too little water going over simply to shoot it. Two more portages brought me to the mouth of the river at Christchurch, where I paused to buy a few supplies and fill my water bottle. After that I headed out to sea and turned right.

The swell of the waves under my kayak was exhilarating and the stress of the exams fell away as I paddled steadily along the coast, about a quarter of a mile offshore. Nobody took any notice of me as I passed Bournemouth, with the entrance to Poole harbour ahead of me as the sun reached the western horizon. I had to dodge a ferry and a couple of small freighters as I crossed the channel that led into the harbour and, as darkness descended, I went ashore in Studland Bay and made camp on the beach for the night.

Sunrise woke me, and I was back on the water early in the morning. Heading south for Swanage, I was overtaken by three paddlers coming fast from the harbour entrance and heading the same way. They were Royal Marines, and I knew a couple of them from competitions we had attended together. They were making a fast transit to Kimmeridge Bay. There they were supposed to loiter for the day and in the evening, make a clandestine landing around the point in Hobarrow Bay. This was part of a military exercise already in progress. Their task was to set up a reconnaissance post ahead of a seaborne landing by troops who would arrive in tank landing craft at dawn the following day.

It was good to have company and we chatted as we paddled along. Then one of them had an idea that pulled me into their mission, if only on the periphery. They wanted me to paddle on ahead, swinging wide and making as if I was heading for a landing below the derelict village of Tyneham. With a bit of luck, any observer on shore would take me for the reconnaissance, especially if I wore military uniform. Meanwhile, the marines would remain very close to the cliffs and make their landing further east, hopefully unobserved.

Before we got to St Aldhelm's Head, we paused and exchanged kit. When we continued, I headed out directly across the bay. Twenty minutes, later the marines crept round the headland close among the waves breaking on the rocks at the bottom of the cliffs. As I approached the shore below Tyneham, I caught sight of figures moving about, so I turned seawards and headed further west, approaching the coast and veering off twice more, as if looking for a secluded spot to go ashore.

Although it couldn't have been easy for a casual observer to see a single canoeist in a dark blue kayak on the vast empty expanse of the rolling sea, I knew I was being watched. The occasional flash of light reflecting off a binocular lens, and fleeting movements among the bushes and along the cliff tops confirmed this. By afternoon, the sea was getting up and I had to work a bit

The rock arch of Durdle Door looks like a huge dragon, leaning into the sea to drink. On the right horizon is St Aldhelm's Head.

harder. I had eaten my dry rations and almost emptied my water bottle, so I decided it was time to go ashore. The marines would have made their landing by now, so my part as decoy was done. I moved close inshore and paddled hard for Lulworth Cove.

Entering through the narrow opening, the cove opens into a circular bay a few hundred yards across, backed by cliffs of the Jurassic coast. At one point, where a small valley descends to the cove, there were a few houses, a small hotel and a café by a bubbling freshwater stream. The café was closing up for the day as I came ashore, but a van selling fish and chips provided me with plentiful starchy sustenance and the stream with water to refill my bottle. After eating, I paddled around to the eastern side of the cove and settled myself for the night among the rocks in a spot impossible to approach except from the water.

In the early morning, the sea was calm enough for me to paddle through Durdle Door. This is a large limestone arch with one foot in the sea, which looks as if a huge dragon is squatting on the shore, leaning out into the water to drink. The formation's strata stand vertically in places. This is more obvious on the eastern side, just as you come out of Lulworth Cove, but from any angle it was a fascinating place.

I paddled west and by late morning had reached Weymouth. I'd had plenty of time to think about things as I paddled across Weymouth Bay, and had decided it might be wise to call the school and let them know where I was. Someone was bound to have noticed after two days that I was absent.

They hadn't noticed.

My call came as a surprise to my housemaster, who had been invigilating another exam at the time of my departure. He told me to stay where I was and wait for someone to collect me. This didn't appeal, so I told him I was already on my way back and ended the call. Then I bought a few supplies from a seafront shop, refilling my water bottle from a public fountain, got back in my canoe and headed east.

The tide was with me and I made St Aldhelm's Head well before dark. A lone figure on the headland standing and waving beside a small green car told me that Mr Frewer had still come looking for me despite my assurance that I was on my way back. Ignoring him, I paddled on.

With the tide now slack, the sea unusually calm, and a clear night in prospect, I moved closer inshore and continued until I had reached the spot on Studland Bay where I had camped before. I slept well on the beach that night, was up early, and made landfall again just west of Christchurch. I had decided the entry through Christchurch harbour to the River Stour offered too many interception points, so I lifted my kayak out of the water, slung it on my shoulder and carried it around the outskirts of the town to a point just upstream. I made steady going up river without interruption, apart from the weirs.

Guessing someone would probably be waiting for me at the canoe shed, I hauled it out of the water down near the woodwork shed and stowed it behind a stack of seasoning planks. It wasn't difficult to get back into the main building unobserved and I managed to have a long hot bath, get dressed and downstairs in time for the evening meal before anyone saw me. It was a house prefect who tapped me on the shoulder and said, "Bod wants to see you after supper. What have you done now to upset him?" Bod was our name for our housemaster.

"Nothing much. I just pissed off for a couple of days after the last exam without asking permission first."

"Oh," he sounded almost disappointed. "By the look on his face, I thought you'd screwed his daughter. Take care, he's in a shitty mood and looking for blood."

Mike Frewer had calmed down a bit by the time I presented myself at his study. I received a long lecture about responsibility and the necessity of telling someone if I was going to absent myself during term time because the school had a duty of care and had to be able to account for the presence and safety of every pupil. He was unimpressed that nobody else had noticed I was missing, and said this gave me no excuse. He had been obliged to report my absconding to the headmaster, who would undoubtedly want to see me. Until he did, I was confined to the immediate surroundings of the main school buildings and under no circumstances was I to go anywhere near the river.

Three days later, the headmaster gave me a similar lecture. He made it clear that if I couldn't toe the line, he would have no compunction about putting me out on my ear, regardless of the consequences that might have to my future prospects. On that note, he asked what my intentions were. Had I decided on a career yet? I muttered something about considering going to an agricultural college, which he thought would be eminently suitable, since no building would be able to contain me. After a tense twenty minutes, we parted in a state of armed neutrality, me to try and find ways of curbing my impulsive behaviour, he ready to throw the book and everything else at me if I stepped out of line again.

As I opened the door to leave, he was gracious enough to congratulate me on the CCF having won a commendation after an inspection visit by the commanding brigadier. As the senior cadet, I'd been largely responsible for driving up the drill standards, map-reading skills and discipline – an interesting irony, considering I'd just been thoroughly berated over my own indiscipline.

32 ~ Per ardua ad astra

THE EXAM RESULTS CAME and I had passed ten subjects, one of them – surprisingly – history. Unfortunately I'd failed the mathematics which I so badly needed for the RAF and knew I would have to retake it.

For my A Level subjects, I chose botany and geography, because they were interesting, and French because I found it easy. My choices caused consternation and intensive enquiries: what did I intend to use these for? The suggestion about agricultural college that I had given evasively to the headmaster came back to haunt me. Which colleges, they wanted to know, and more to the point right now, how would the subjects I was choosing be relevant when those colleges were all asking for different ones? I mumbled something about doing tropical agriculture but the response was the same.

Reluctantly, I agreed to reconsider and asked permission to go and visit a couple of colleges. That request was surprisingly well-received and permission was granted, but I'd have to arrange the visits myself.

This was music to my ears: I'd sent off my forms to the RAF

and they'd already called me for a selection panel. So I told the school those dates and said I'd spend that time visiting three colleges. Fortunately nobody at the school bothered to contact my parents about this, as I'd said nothing to them. Dad's posting in Nigeria had ended in 1964 and he'd been posted back to a staff job in Southern Command Headquarters at Wilton in Wiltshire. This meant he was close enough to interfere if he thought it necessary.

By the time he did learn about it, I'd been accepted for pilot training. The first he knew was when an RAF security officer called at the house to interview my mother. On the application forms, one of the background questions about my family had asked my mother's age. I'd put down thirty-nine, because that's what she always said if anyone asked her age. My brother, when he joined the RAF four years earlier, had done the same. Some bright clerk had picked up the anomaly and sent an officer to check.

Dad caught on quickly.

"So how old is your wife then, sir?" the officer asked.

"Thirty-nine," he replied.

The security officer was suitably confused and pressed the question, at which point Dad suggested he should go into the kitchen and ask her himself. Discretion being the better part of valour, the investigator closed his folder and departed.

The inquisition started when I came home from school for a weekend and didn't really let up until a letter arrived giving the date on which I was to report to No 2 Officer Training School at RAF South Cerney. At that point, Dad recognised that I too wasn't going to join his regiment.

ON PARADE THE DAY I joined up, the flight sergeant moved down the ranks, asked each man his name. When he got to me, he asked what age my mother was. A slight twist of his lips when I said thirty-nine told me he already knew a lot about me. His second question surprised me and confirmed this: he demanded to know why I didn't have my medal ribbon on my uniform.

"Medal ribbon, Flight Sergeant?" I enquired

"You were given a Coronation Medal. That wasn't just a pretty bauble," he snapped. "You should show some respect. Get the ribbon on your uniform by tomorrow."

I'd forgotten all about it, and hadn't seen the gong for years.

That evening in the mess, one of the other recruits asked about the medal and I told him how it had come to be awarded. After that, the conversation somehow got onto school transport and I started recounting the story of the school bus and the man-eating leopard. I'd just reached the point where the farmer came back to his Land Rover with the dead leopard over his shoulders when I paused to take a swig from my pint. A smooth velvety voice behind my shoulder carried on with exactly the same words I was about to use. The hairs on my neck stood up.

Turning around, I saw a grinning black face I hadn't seen for twelve years, since we shared a bench at the mission school. It was Gilbert Chileshe, the boy into whose family I had been adopted and initiated. He had joined the Zambian Air Force and had been sent to Britain for training with us.

We retired from the group to catch up on the intervening years. The Chinyanja language, unused for all that time, came flooding back. Our companions were left wondering what we were jabbering about.

Fortunately Gilbert had some medal ribbon, so the two of us turned up properly dressed on parade the following morning.

For the next twelve weeks, we hardly had time to think. There was a great deal of square bashing and long sessions in the gymnasium to get us really fit, together with runs around the airfield carrying packs loaded with bricks. Many military establishments used this activity as punishment, but as aircrew we had to reach and maintain a high standard of fitness. The intensive programme was designed to achieve this before the end of our three-month officer training course. We also had classroom lectures on everything from Air Force history to current deployment structures, discipline and decorum, to rank and responsibilities, orders and instructions, Queen's Regulations and Air Force law.

Weapons training started after two months. At the range, we handled a variety of weapons from rifles to sub-machine guns and pistols. With my Army and bush background, I was already a decent shot and surprised the instructor by hitting a cigarette packet at fifteen yards with eight out of nine rounds in the pistol. But the best shot with a rifle was Gilbert. He was also the most adept at dismantling and reassembling weapons; being the son of an armourer gave him something of an advantage.

Gilbert had always been accurate with a slingshot too. When I commented on this, the weapons officer laughed and said it wouldn't be much use in a military situation. So I took the laces out of my boots and, using a folded handkerchief to make the cup, I fashioned a sling. We picked a stone at random from the ground as the projectile and a few minutes later Gilbert showed him that his slingshot was more accurate and had more stopping power at forty yards than the instructor could achieve with his 9mm Browning pistol.

The week after weapons training, we went to a camp in the Brecon Beacons for a ten-day romp in the hills. For the first four days, we had an escape and evasion exercise on Mynyydd

Llangattog, a large flat plateau to the south of the Beacons. As luck would have it, this was an area I knew well, having visited it a number of times to go caving. Avoiding capture there was not difficult. The limestone plateau was riddled with caves, some extending to several miles of passages. Our flight simply hid in one of the less accessible caves for three days and then sneaked down to the reporting point during the night, just before the exercise was due to end. We were finally spotted by a patrol of the Royal Welsh Regiment on our final approach and had to make a mad dash for the safety of the reporting tent. We were the only flight not caught.

We spent the following week yomping over the mountains with a night exercise at the end of it. Besides Gilbert, there were three other African students and three Jordanians on our course. The staff had noticed early on that I got on well with the Africans, so we were assigned to the same flight and given the task of establishing and defending a position against the rest of the squadron, who would invade at some point during the night and attempt to capture our prize. The prize was a life-sized poster of Marilyn Monroe, pasted to a board.

Besides the trophy, we were issued with ration packs, an old green parachute, a few lengths of parachute cord and a machete. We also managed to acquire some flares and a number of thunderflashes, but kept quiet about them. Basically very large penny bangers, they go off with a satisfying bang and can make the ears ring for a few hours if you're standing too close when they detonate.

Scanning the one-inch map, we selected a small copse with space all round it and a gully leading away downhill for our camp and left immediately after lunch to establish ourselves.

On the way up the mountain, we came across an injured sheep and quickly despatched it with a knife. While the ration packs were all right to survive on, we had no intention of being uncomfortable and our Jordanians, bemused by the whole business up to this point, suddenly came to life at the prospect of fresh meat. When we reached the copse, they volunteered to cook while we Africans set up a defensive perimeter. By sunset, we were ready to repel intruders. We had a comfortable camp, a good meal inside us, a formidable defensive perimeter and a night of fun to look forward to.

The fun began unexpectedly just before midnight when one of the staff, acting as an umpire, wandered into our camp and sprung a trap. We had ringed the camp with bush traps. The one he walked into consisted of a ground noose and a springy sapling. One moment he was walking forward into the copse, and the next he was suspended in the air by one leg, yelling like there was no tomorrow. Danson Kamotho, one of the Kenyans, immediately started whacking at him with a long pole, hissing "Shut up, or a'am going to beat you!"

"Get me down from here!" bellowed the umpire.

"No! If you don' shut up, a'am going to beat you more," hissed Danson, applying his stick again.

"Is that you, Kamotho?" demanded the outraged umpire. "I can't see you."

"Daa's because a'am black and is dark. Now shut up or I beat you more!" Danson was not to be messed with and gave the suspended figure another hefty whack for good measure.

The rest of us were doubled up laughing as we came to help lower our captive to the ground. As soon as we could reach him, Gilbert stuffed a gag round his mouth and secured it with cargo tape. We then bound him to a tree next to our tent and left him there to watch what happened.

Danson and Gilbert reset the trap which had proved so successful.

The umpire, Flight Lieutenant Pemberton, had been carrying a portable radio which he'd dropped when the trap sprung. When it chirped, we picked it up and were able to listen to the other umpires chatting about how the exercise was proceeding. They obviously noticed that Uniform Six was off air and not responding, but assumed it was simply radio failure, and so continued to chat freely, unaware that we were listening. With this advantage, we were well-briefed and ready to repel the squadron by the time the attack eventually came. Our captive umpire was clearly very unhappy about all this but, still trussed and bound to his tree, could do nothing about it and every noise he made simply earned him another clout from Danson's stick.

At the end of the exercise, we still had Marilyn Monroe, together with nine other prisoners caught in our traps. The other umpires told us off for capturing and holding one of their number, but when we explained how it had come about, we knew they were amused and Flt Lt Pemberton would take a long time to live it down in the mess. I met him a few years later and he still blushed at the memory.

We came back from the exercise to hear there had been an accident at the base camp. One of the cadets had crossed a safety line and fallen twenty-five feet down a steep riverbank during the night. His head had collided with a rock as he fell, killing him instantly. There was little laughter as we packed up the camp and prepared to return to South Cerney.

It was 0500 when we got back to the station. We disembarked

from our buses straight into the drill hangar to learn the drill for a military funeral. At 09.30, we changed into our smart uniforms and marched off to form a guard of honour at the village church.

We buried our comrade with full military ceremony and fired volleys over his grave. It was a sad day.

Three days later, we were on parade again, this time for our course's passing out parade. Mum and Dad came down to do the proud parents bit, and my brother also managed to attend. Mum took the only photograph we have of the three of us in uniform together.

After the parade, the Flight Sergeant approached, saluted and shook my hand. Then he said, "Please sir, next time we have a parade will you not show me up by appearing improperly dressed?"

"Improperly dressed, Flight?"

"Yes sir, you forgot your bloody medal again!"

WHILE THE OTHER NEW officers went off to basic flying school, I was sent to a holding post. I already had a private pilot's licence and four hundred hours in my logbook. While the others did the basic course, I spent three months flying Chipmunks, taking Air Cadets for air experience flights. It was an ideal opportunity to polish my own basic skills and do lots of aerobatics. All too soon it came to an end and I was posted to RAF Syerston, near Newark in Nottinghamshire, to learn to fly jets.

Flying training was fun and I revelled in every minute of it. The whole process of flight took on all sorts of new dimensions as we learned the science behind flight along with the skills necessary to handle any and every situation that might present itself in the air. Ground school was equally interesting as we learned about the

Despite the fact that we had deserted the Army in favour of the RAF, Dad was proud to have both sons in the service.

aircraft and the mechanisms, systems and processes that kept us in the air. There were the flight rules, radio procedures, meteorology and navigation to learn, along with aviation medicine and the effects of gravity, altitude and oxygen starvation on the human body. Our instructors expected high professional standards in everything we did.

Training never stops when you're a pilot, even on the ground; there are constant performance checks and new systems to learn with different aircraft, weapons and navigational aids. You spend a lot of time in a simulator, but the time you spend in the air is special, particularly in a single-seat aircraft. I harboured ambitions to go on and fly helicopters or some of the big maritime patrol aircraft, but fate turned me in a different direction.

33 ~ Back to Africa

THE UK GOVERNMENT OF the day, run by Harold Wilson, considered defence a burden to the tax-payer. They preferred to spend the national revenue on nanny-state policies and inefficient, loss-making nationalised industries. To this end, Wilson instituted a series of cuts to the defence budget, and a lot of aircrew found themselves grounded.

In those days, a flying posting carried an additional ten shillings a day in pay, so reducing aircrew numbers was an easy way to make savings. At first this affected mainly older men, but gradually the net tightened as the politicians realised their criteria were too loose. Some bright spark decided all aircrew with an A2 medical grading should be grounded as they were not as fit as those with A1. Actually it meant they had received treatment in an RAF hospital and were fully fit for everything, but politicians are not noted for understanding, or choosing to understand, what they are dealing with. To them '2' was inferior to '1'.

I'd had my sinuses bored out in the hospital at RAF Halton, so this bracket caught me. Grounded and sent to the RAF selection centre at Biggin Hill, I found myself trying to teach French and RAF history to bored WRAFs, and taking frequent turns as duty dog because there was only a handful of junior officers on the station.

Before long, it became apparent that I wasn't going to get back to flying without some heavyweight assistance, so I asked to speak to the AOC. He listened patiently to my plea but said that, as this was a political decision and not a military one, his hands were tied. While he sympathised with my situation and agreed that after all the money the RAF had spent training me, I should be in the air, he could do nothing. A number of opportunities in radar control and administrative functions might be open to me. But that was all he could offer.

If I couldn't fly, I didn't want to be part of the Air Force, so I asked to resign my commission. He accepted. Two days later, when I was handing in my kit, I met him doing the same thing.

I wasn't sure what to do next, so I went to spend a few days with my parents who were then living in Maidenhead as Dad had another posting in the Ministry of Defence. We hadn't seen each other for some months, so it was good to catch up. It also offered me a base from which to explore other opportunities. In the end, I didn't have to look far as the opportunity sought me out.

The morning after I arrived in Maidenhead, the door bell rang and a grey little man in a dull grey suit asked to speak to me. He was indeed diminutive and looked unremarkable, but soon showed that he had steel in him. He explained that he worked for a department of the Foreign Office and was aware of my situation. It had been noticed, during my time in the RAF, that I got on particularly well with the African cadets and officers, and that I had a command of several African languages. His department, he said, needed people like me to work in the field.

He clearly knew how to lay out the right bait, for within an hour I had agreed to go up to London the following day and talk to someone else. Before he left, he presented me with a copy of an official document and asked me to read and sign it.

"I've already signed the Official Secrets Act," I said, looking at the title.

"And you'll do so many more times before you're finished, so sign it."

I signed.

"Good. You now belong to us. You may not tell anyone, and that includes your family, what you're doing. You'll be given some training and I'd expect to see you out in Africa in about six months time. Your appointment is for 09.30 tomorrow. Don't be late." He handed me a small card with an address and a telephone number on it.

I went to London and did the training, which included a number of short specialist courses and an intensive management training programme with one of the Unilever companies. As part of this programme, to gain some experience of industrial work, I was put in charge of a team of fitters working in Widnes, Runcorn, the Wirral and south Liverpool. They were gas fitters, converting domestic properties from the old town gas supply to the new natural gas system that was then being introduced.

We moved across the sector, house by house, street by street, a crew of eight men converting all the gas-fired appliances in about a thousand properties a week. Some only had a cooker in them, but many had gas fires, back boilers, water heaters, central heating systems and other appliances as well. All of these had to be fitted with new nozzles, burners and pressure regulators and made to burn cleanly. Many of the cookers were filthy, some even crawling with maggots, and a few were so old that the parts had not been produced to convert them. For these we had to seal the old jets with silver solder and then drill new ones with microfine bits, cobbling together pressure regulators off other appliances.

It was challenging and interesting work and, to add spice, the men in my crew were a varied bunch with a lively and provocative sense of humour. Their favourite topics of conversation were sex, football and beer. At lunchtime, their preferred diet was a huge packet of chips with curry sauce and mushy peas, so they always asked for the crew van, which also served as a workshop, to be parked as near as possible to the neighbourhood chippy.

The interlude was all too brief. Five months later, I found myself back in London for two weeks of final briefings before boarding a plane to West Africa.

It was after dark when the plane landed. The aircraft door was opened before we reached our stand by the terminal, allowing the warm evening air to flow in. With it came the familiar smells of foetid vegetation, half-burned jet fuel and the unmistakable stale urine odour of termites. To me, it smelled like nectar.

It told me I was home. It was the smell of freedom.

Glossary

askari – an African soldier.

awdgalu – a crested crane. The plural is *zingaru*.

ayah – child's nursemaid.

bac mòno – a peat bank, from which household fuel (peat) is cut in slabs and stacked to dry in the breeze.

bairn – baby, child.

biddy – a woman, especially an old one, regarded as annoying or interfering.

biltong – sun-dried, and often smoked, strips of meat.

boma – a thorny fence around a campsite, to keep unwanted visitors out.

broch – a derelict prehistoric stone dwelling in Scotland.

chai – Indian sweetened boiled tea, offered to us by traders in the Aden bazaars.

chele salondola – answer your name!

chongololo – a big black millipede, anything up to eight inches long and as thick as a man's thumb.

doki boy – A groom. Literally *horse boy*, one who looks after horses.

driech – dull, dreary, bleak.

howk – dig up.

induna – leader or captain of a traditional military formation.

jaali – a net cover with a weighted fringe, which could be put over jugs or bowls to keep flies off food.

kalilombe – chamæleon.

kopje – a rocky outcrop forming a large hill. The one on the road to school had a cleft, though which the road ran.

kirk – church, the Kirk of Scotland.

mealies – maize; **mealie** – a corn cob.

messages – errands, general shopping.

monguus – mongoose. The name by which we referred to the Mother Superior at the mission school, because of her mongoose-like features.

mupfura fruits – also called **Marula**. These plum-sized fruits are yellow when ripe and have creamy white flesh around a walnut-sized pip. Highly prized both for their tart flesh and for their nutty seeds, they are particular favourites of elephants and giraffes, the former often damaging the trees in their eagerness to get at ripe fruit.

msuzi – soup.

naartjies – (pronounced *narchees*) tangerines.

ndio – yes. Also used as a catch-all acknowledgement.

nganga – witch doctor.

posho – thick grey millet porridge.

rondavel – a traditional African round hut, with mud walls and a conical thatched roof.

sadza – stiff maize porridge.

Sarkin Zazzau – the traditional title of the Emir of Zaria.

sleaghdn – (pronounced *slane*) a peat cutting knife, used to cut fuel on **bac mòno** (*qv*). There are several different forms.

totos – young (elephants, or humans).

Acknowledgements

IAN ALWAYS GENEROUSLY acknowledged other people's contributions, particularly to anything he was involved in directly, including his books. I know he would want to mention all those who helped in the development of this book, so I am saying thank you for him. I also want to add my own special thanks to Chuck Grieve of Mosaïque Press who guided me through this process and to Ian's lifelong friend John McFarlane for sharing his memories and also his meticulous attention to detail.

– GM

■ Visit www.ianmathie.co.uk for information about the author and his books and links to interviews, reviews and other writing by Ian Mathie.

Lightning Source UK Ltd.
Milton Keynes UK
UKHW020543100519
342448UK00006B/94/P